Table of Contents

Introduction

The Praxis II: Elementary Education Multiple Subjects Exam is designed to prepare elementary teachers for the classroom by ensuring that they have a strong knowledge base in the four core content areas that they will be expected to teach. These core content areas are Reading/Language Arts, Mathematics, Social Studies, and Science.

The Test at a Glance

Test Code	5031		
Format	Multiple choice only		
Total Time	3.5 hours (four separately timed subtests- see below)		
Method of Delivery	Computer		
Permitted Tools	Scientific or four-function calculator		
Subtests	*Subtest*	*Time Allowed*	*# of Questions*
	Reading/Language Arts	60 minutes	65
	Mathematics	50 minutes	40
	Social Studies	50 minutes	55
	Science	50 minutes	50

Each of these subtests has multiple component subheadings and standards that will be explored in the rest of this guide.

Reading and Language Arts

Reading and language arts are foundational for student success. Students develop skills in reading, writing, and speaking that demonstrate comprehension of written and spoken texts, a command of the mechanics of the English language, and critical thinking skills.

Test Structure

The Reading/ Language Arts subtest is the largest section of the overall exam. It consists of 65 multiple choice questions and lasts one hour. Within Reading/ Language Arts, there are two major subcategories with which you must be familiar:

A. Reading (49% of the Reading/ Language Arts content)

B. Language, Writing, and Communication (51% of the Reading/Language Arts content)

Each subcategory is divided into standards, which state the skills you must be able to demonstrate on the exam.

Reading

The Reading section covers literacy development and the understanding of the elements of fiction and non-fiction texts.

Standards Addressed:

A. Foundational Skills

1. The Foundations of Literacy and Reading Development
2. The Role of Phonological Awareness and Phonics in Literacy Development
3. The Role of Fluency in Supporting Comprehension
4. The Stages of Early Orthographic Development

B. Literature and Informational Texts

1. The Role of Comprehension
2. The Basic Elements of Literature and Informational Texts
3. The Basic Elements of Poetry and Drama
4. Literary Terms and Figurative Language

Foundational Skills

The Foundations of Literacy and Reading Development

The foundations of literacy are those early stages during which students gain the basic literacy skills that will be the building blocks for their future reading and writing. It is important to support these foundations because gaining these skills early in life sets students up to be more successful throughout their future.

Foundations of Literacy

- **Emergent Literacy**

  Emergent literacy refers to the language development that occurs before a child can read or write words. These skills are developed from birth and include listening, speaking, memory, recognizing pattern and rhyme, print awareness, critical thinking, and the development of the fine motor skills necessary for writing.

- **Concept of Print**

  Understanding the concept of print is the awareness that written letters have sounds and that they form words.

- **Letter Knowledge**

  Basic knowledge of the alphabet and what sounds each letter makes is foundational for literacy acquisition.

- **Logographic Foundation**

  Logographic reading is the reading of sight words, which involves the use of visual cues.

- **Phonetic Reading**

  Phonetic reading uses letter-sound correspondence as a first step in simple decoding. Learners must understand what the letters are and what sounds they make.

Promoting Literacy Development in Second-Language Learners

Depending on the individual student, second-language learners may have varying degrees of literacy both in their native language and in English. Some basic principles to promote successful literacy for these students are:

- Place value on the literacy skills they already possess, including those in their native language.

- Utilize and enrich first-language knowledge.

- Ensure that English as Second Language (ESL) instruction is at a developmentally appropriate level but is also age-appropriate and challenging enough to maintain interest.

- Provide explicit vocabulary instruction.

- Provide ample exposure to rich language input.

- Maintain open communication, provide positive feedback, and encourage peer relationships.

Phonological awareness is the understanding that words are made up of sound units (called "phonemes"). **Phonics** is the understanding the sounds and printed letters are connected. The two concepts together make up the foundation for the reading process.

There are several skills that make up each of these areas and are important to the development of early literacy.

Phonological Awareness Skills:

- **Rhyming**- having an ending sound that corresponds with another (e.g. *cat, hat*)

- **Segmenting**- the ability to break a word up into its individual component sounds

Phonics Skills:

- **Alphabetic Principle**- the understanding that words are made up of letters that have different sounds

- **Letter-Sound Correspondence**- the knowledge of the sounds that are associated with each letter of the alphabet

- **Decoding**- the ability to apply the knowledge of letter-sound relationships in order to pronounce written words. Decoding requires several skills of its own. To successfully decode a word, a learner must be able to know the letters in the word and their appropriate sounds, remember each of these sounds in sequence, and put the sounds together to create a word.

- **Syllabication**- the ability to correctly divide words into syllables

Fluency is the ability to read text smoothly, without paying much conscious attention to the mechanics of reading. As learners' literacy skills develop, their fluency increases over time. Whereas beginning readers must decode and sound out many words, fluent readers give no thought to this and are able to read with speed and accuracy. Once readers become more fluent and no longer have to spending their time and mental energy decoding words, they can focus more on comprehension.

Fluency is measured by two main components—rate and accuracy.

- **Rate**- the speed at which reading occurs
- **Accuracy**- a measure of the percentage of oral reading that is correct

The Stages of Early Orthographic Development

As children grow and develop, so do their writing skills. From their earliest scrawling eventually develops fully written compositions. Teachers should be familiar with how this process unfolds.

Stage	Description
Drawing	Expresses ideas through pictures; uses drawing as a form of communication
Scribbles	Uses scribbles as a form of writing; intends the scribbles to have meaning like writing
Letter-like Forms	Shapes start to look like letters but are not actual letters
Random letters	Writes actual letters but in patterns or strings that make no sense
Invented spelling	Begins to form words but with own spelling; sometimes phonetic spelling; sometimes a single letter may stand for syllables or whole words; improves over time
Conventional spelling	Spells correctly and resembles adult writing

Comprehension is the ability to understand read content, process it, and think about it critically. Comprehension takes reading beyond fluency— which just requires words to be pronounced correctly and fluidly—and into a process in which the words take on deeper meaning.

Types of Comprehension

There are two main types of reading comprehension—literal and critical.

Literal comprehension is understanding of the meaning of the words in a passage. This can include tasks like:

- Stating the main idea of a passage
- Identifying out the topic sentence of a passage
- Identifying supporting details

Critical comprehension employs reasoning to infer deeper meanings and draw conclusions not directly stated in a passage.

This can include tasks like:

- Determining the author's purpose and tone
- Distinguishing fact from opinion
- Recognizing bias
- Drawing logical inferences and conclusions

Strategies for Comprehension

There are many strategies students can employ to increase their reading comprehension. Here are several common ones:

- Annotating texts

- Drawing on prior knowledge to make inferences, make connections, and draw conclusions (also called inferential reading)

- Metacognition—awareness of one's own knowledge; self-monitoring to assess progress, identify difficulties, and employ strategic problem-solving

- Multi-pass strategies such as SQ3R (Survey, Question, Read, Recite, Review)

- Pre- and post-reading exercises such as K-W-L (Know, Want to Know, Learned)

- Summarizing

- Using graphic organizers

There are many types of literature written for children. They fall under two general categories—fiction and non-fiction. **Fiction** is material that not an accurate account of real people and events but rather is imagined by the author. **Non-fiction** is material that is presented as being factual and accurate.

Major Types of Literature

The major forms of fiction and non-fiction literature include, but are not limited to, those listed in the chart that follows:

Fiction	Non-Fiction
• Allegory- story in which the characters and events represent ideas or concepts • Drama (play)- a piece meant for performance, where the story is presented through dialogue • Fable- a short story with a moral lesson • Folktale- a story passed down through oral traditions • Myth- a story created to explain natural or social phenomena • Novel- a book-length narrative that presents its characters and plot with a degree of realism • Parable- a short story used to teach a moral lesson • Short story- a brief work of narrative prose • Tall tale- an exaggerated story, usually about a real person	• Autobiography- an account of the author's own life • Biography- an account of another person's life • Diary (or journal)- a dated, personal record of events over a period of time • Essay- a short piece intended to express an author's point of view on a topic • Letter- written correspondence from one person to another • Textbook-a book used to study a particular subject

Poetry is a form of creative literature written in verse. Poetry can take many forms, several of which are listed in the chart below:

Form	Definition
Acrostic	A poem in which the first letter of each line forms a word when read from top to bottom
Ballad	A poem narrating a story in stanzas, often quatrains
Blank Verse	Poetry that is metered but not rhymed
Cinquain	A five line poem with specified syllabic emphasis, depending on the type of cinquain
Concrete	A poem written into a familiar shape relating to the poem's meaning
Elegy	A poem about someone's death
Epic	A long poem about the adventures of a hero
Free Verse	Poetry that is neither rhymed nor metered
Haiku	A Japanese form of poetry that contains three lines of 5, 7, and 5 syllables, in that order
Limerick	A humorous five-line poem with a rhyme scheme of AABBA
Lyric	A poem expressing personal emotions
Ode	A lyric poem addressed to a particular subject, which often contains lofty imagery
Sonnet	A fourteen-line poem

Poetry also has its own unique vocabulary of terms, including techniques that poets employ in creating their works.

Term	Definition	Example	
Alliteration	Repetition of a beginning consonant sound	"Peter Piper picked a peck of pickled peppers."	
Assonance	Repetition of vowel sounds	"As I was going to St. Ives, I met a man with seven wives."	
Consonance	Repetition of consonant sounds anywhere in the words	"Hickory, Dickory, Dock, The mouse ran up the clock. The clock struck one, The mouse ran down. Hickory, Dickory, Dock."	
Foot	One unit of meter	**Type of Foot**	**Definition**
		Iambic	Unstressed syllable followed by a stressed syllable
		Trochaic	Stressed syllable followed by an unstressed syllable
		Spondaic	Two stressed syllables in a row
		Pyrrhic	Two unstressed syllables in a row
		Anapestic	Two unstressed syllables followed by a stressed syllable
		Dactylic	Stressed syllable followed by two unstressed syllables
Meter	The rhythm of a poem, dependent on the number of syllables and how they are accented		
Mood	A poem's feeling or atmosphere		

Term	Definition	Example	
Repetition	Using a word or phrase more than once for rhythm or emphasis	"Show men dutiful? Why, so didst thou: seem they grave and learned? Why, so didst thou: come they of noble family? Why, so didst thou: seem they religious? Why, so didst thou."	
Rhyme	The repetition of ending word sounds; can be *internal rhyme* (within a line) or *end rhyme* (the words at the end of the lines rhyme with each other)	Internal rhyme: "Jack Sprat could eat no fat." End rhyme: "Little Miss Muffet Sat on a tuffet"	
Rhythm	The pattern of sounds with a poem		
Stanza	Groups of lines of poetry; named for how many lines they contain	*Name*	*# of Lines*
		Couplet	2
		Triplet	3
		Quatrain	4
		Quintain	5
		Sestet	6
		Septet	7
		Octane	8
Verse	A line of metered poetry; named for the number of feet per line	*Name*	*# of Feet*
		Monometer	1
		Dimeter	2
		Trimeter	3
		Tertameter	4
		Pentameter	5
		Hexameter	6
		Heptameter	7
		Octometer	8

Drama is a literary form in which the story is presented through dialogue and is meant to be performed for an audience. Common forms of drama intended for children include:

- Plays
- Skits
- Puppetry
- Story theater

Figurative language is writing that goes beyond the literal meaning of the words and uses comparison to convey meaning.

Term	Definition	Example
Alliteration	Repetition of a beginning consonant sound; considered figurative language because it can help create mood and imagery	The lonesome lady left one last, long, look for her love.
Hyperbole	Exaggeration for emphasis	I'm so hungry I could eat a whole elephant!
Idiom	A phrase that has come to have a different meaning through usage than the meanings of its individual words	Something easy is said to be "a piece of cake."
Imagery	Descriptive writing that appeals to the senses	The rich aroma of coffee drifted through the air, bringing warmth on a bitter January morning.
Metaphor	A comparison between two things that does not use "like" or "as"	He is a chicken.
Onomatopoeia	Words that convey sounds	Buzz, crackle, pop, bang
Oxymoron	Combining two words with opposite meanings	Jumbo shrimp
Personification	Giving human characteristics to nonhuman things	The leaves danced as the wind whistled through the trees.
Simile	A comparison between two things that uses "like" or "as"	Cool as a cucumber

Language, Writing, and Communication

Understanding the elements of language enables learners to effectively express meaning through the written word. Communication skills such as writing, speaking, listening, and viewing are also essential components of language arts.

Standards Addressed:

A. Language

1. The Components of Written Language

2. Sentence Types and Sentence Structure

3. The Basic Components of Vocabulary

B. Writing

1. The Types and Traits of Writing

2. The Stages of The Writing Process

3. Structures and Organization of Writing

4. The Use of Resource Materials in Reading and Language Arts

C. Communication

1. Aspects of Speaking

2. Aspects of Listening

3. Aspects of Viewing

4. The Role of Speaking, Listening, and Viewing in Language Acquisition for Second Language Learners

Language

The Components of Written Language

The main components of written language are grammar, usage, and syntax. **Grammar** is the set of guidelines which govern the proper use of language. **Usage** refers to the proper use of words. **Syntax** is the manner in which words are arranged into sentences.

Parts of Speech

The basic types of words which make up the English language are known as parts of speech.

Part of Speech	Definition	Examples
Noun	Person, place, thing, or idea	boy, ball, Utah, democracy
Pronoun	Word that can take the place of a noun	he, it, something
Verb	Word that reflects an action or state of being	run, be
Adverb	A word that modifies a verb	quickly, very
Adjective	Descriptive word	happy, cold
Preposition	A word that indicates direction or position, or connects two ideas	on, off, above, to, of, from, at
Article	A word that comes before a noun that indicates whether the noun is specific or non-specific	a, an, the, this
Conjunction	A words that joins two words or phrases	for, and, nor, but, or, yet, so

Nouns

There are several different ways to classify nouns.

- Common vs. Proper

    o **Common noun**- general thing or idea; does not require capitalization. Examples: girl, country, religion

    o **Proper noun**- refers to a specific person, place, thing, or idea and DOES require capitalization. Examples: Alicia, Canada, Buddhism

- Singular vs. Plural

    o **Singular**- refers to only one thing. Examples: apple, goose

    o **Plural**- refers to more than one thing. Examples: apples, geese

- Subject vs. Object

    o The **subject** of a sentence is who or what the sentence is about. The subject performs the main verb of the sentence.

    o The **object** of a sentence is not the main subject of the sentence and has the verb *performed on it*.

    Example: *"Lisa enjoys listening to music."* In this sentence, "Lisa" is the subject and "music" is the object.

- Concrete vs. Abstract

    o **Concrete noun**- physical object. Examples: rock, building

    o **Abstract noun**- non-physical things, like ideas. Examples: creativity, sadness

Pronouns

Pronouns take the place of more specific nouns. The noun that a pronoun stands for is called the **antecedent.** Example: *"Daniel works as a financial planner. He has worked at the same company for ten years."*

In this example, "he" is the pronoun and "Daniel" is the antecedent.

Just like nouns, pronouns can be classified as subjects or objects.

- Subject pronouns: he, she, I, we, they

- Object pronouns: him, her, me, us, them

Pronouns can also show possession.

- Examples: her, his, my, mine, ours, their

Verbs

There are three major types of verbs—action, linking, and helping.

- **Action verbs** show an action performed by the subject of a sentence.
    - Example: She <u>ran</u> to the store.
- **Linking verbs** connect the subject of the sentence to the additional information about the subject.
    - Example: The cat <u>was</u> black.
- **Helping verbs** are paired with another verb and are often used to indicate tense.
    - Example: School <u>will</u> be open tomorrow.

Verbs also indicate the time period in which the action is taking place. This is called **tense**. There are three major tenses—present, past, and future.

- **Present tense**- the action is occurring now

    Example: Anna lives in New York City.

- **Past tense**- the action occurred in the past

    Example: Anna lived in New York City.

- **Future tense**- the action will occur in the future

    Example: Anna will live in New York City.

Syntax

Syntax is the manner in which words are arranged into sentences. There are rules that govern proper syntax. A sentence must contain both a subject and a predicate.

- **Subject-** the part of the sentence that is *performing* the action; the noun that the sentence is about

  Example: <u>Many trees and bushes</u> grow in the forest.

- **Predicate-** gives information about the subject

  Example: Many trees and bushes <u>grow in the forest.</u>

A sentence *may* also contain one or more objects. As stated above, an object is a noun that receives the action of the verb. Objects can be direct or indirect.

- **Direct object-** directly receives the action of the predicate; answer the questions "whom?" or "what?"

- **Indirect object-** indirectly receives the action of the predicate; answer the questions "to whom/what?" "from whom/what?"

- Example:

  "I gave a treat to the dog."

  Subject- "I"

  Direct object- "treat"

  Indirect object- "dog"

Words are grouped together in several basic forms.

- **Phrases** are the most basic grouping of words. The words are related but may lack a subject (e.g. "went swimming) and/or a predicate (e.g. "my mother").

- **Clauses** are groups of words that contain both a subject and a verb. There are two types of clauses:

  - **Independent clause-** expresses a complete thought and could stand alone as a complete sentence

  - **Dependent clause-** does not express a complete thought and therefore could not stand alone as a complete sentence

- Example:

  "Because he got a flat tire, Tim was late to work."

  "Tim was late to work" is an independent clause because it could stand alone as a complete sentence.

  "Because he got a flat tire" is a dependent clause because it could not stand alone as a complete sentence.

- **Sentences** are groups of words that contain both a subject and a predicate and express a complete thought. There are several different types of sentences, which will be explored in detail later in this section.

A **sentence** is a grammatical structure that includes both a subject and a predicate and expresses a complete thought.

Types of Sentences

There are four main types of sentences:

1. **Declarative-** makes a statement and ends with a period.

   Example: My dog's name is Bruno.

2. **Imperative-** gives a command and usually ends with a period.

   Example: Give me that pencil.

3. **Interrogative-** asks a question and ends with a question mark.

   Example: Will you eat dinner with us tonight?

4. **Exclamatory-** shows strong feeling and ends with an exclamation point.

   Example: I'm so happy to see you!

Sentence Structure

There are four main types of sentence structures:

1. **Simple sentences** contain one independent clause.

   Example: I went to the store.

2. **Compound sentences** contain two or more independent clauses, joined by a conjunction or punctuation mark.

   Example: I went to the store and I bought eggs.

3. **Complex sentences** contain one independent clause and at least one dependent clause.

   Example: On my way home from work, I went to the store.

4. **Compound-complex sentences** contain at least two independent clauses and at least one dependent clause.

   Example: On my way home from work, I went to the store and I bought eggs, then I stopped for gas.

Vocabulary acquisition is an important part of literacy development. As readers mature, they should gain a more extensive vocabulary. There are several tools that can help students to interpret new vocabulary:

- **Affixes**- common beginnings (prefixes) and endings (suffixes) that add meaning to a base word. Understanding the meaning of an affix can help students make sense of the word.

Common Prefixes	Common Suffixes
A-	-er
Bi-	-est
Tri-	-ing
Un-	-ly
Pre-	-fy
Non-	-it
Dis-	-is
Anti-	-tion

- **Root words**- the most basic form of a word that conveys meaning. Many words in the English language have root words from other languages, such as Greek and Latin. There are hundreds of root words in the English language but a few examples are listed in the chart below.

Root Word	Meaning	Example
Aqua	Water	Aquatic
Demo	People	Democracy
Geo	Earth	Geography
Mal	Bad	Malice
Mono	One	Monologue
Poly	Many	Polytheism
Omni	All	Omniscient
Script	Write	Manuscript

- **Context clues**- information in the text surrounding a new word that help provide meaning

Writing

The Types and Traits of Writing

Types of Writing

There are six main genres of writing elementary students may encounter:

1. **Expository Writing:** writing meant to inform

   Examples: research papers, reports, biographies

2. **Narrative Writing:** writing that tells a story

   Examples: novels, short stories, plays

3. **Persuasive Writing:** writing that expresses the author's point of view

   Examples: argumentative essay, editorial, reviews, advertisements

   Journaling/Letter Writing: writing written as a personal message for a specific audience (either themselves or another person or organization)

   Examples: journals/diaries, learning logs, business letters, personal letters, emails

4. **Descriptive Writing:** writing meant to describe someone or something; uses language that appeals to the senses

   Examples: descriptive essays, character sketches

5. **Poetry Writing:** creative writing written in verse

   Examples: any of the types of poetry addressed the Reading section.

Traits of Writing

All writing contains three main traits—tone, purpose, and audience.

1. **Tone-** the feeling or attitude that a piece of writing conveys

   Examples: humorous, sad, serious, uplifting

2. **Purpose-** why the author wrote the piece; what is the goal of this piece of writing?

   Examples: to persuade, to entertain, to inform

3. **Audience-** who the piece is intended for; who is supposed to be reading this?

   Examples: children, adults, women, sports fans

In addition to these general characteristics, narratives have their own set of traits.

- **Setting-** when and where the story takes place

- **Theme-** the underlying idea of a story

- **Plot-** the events in the story; there are five parts to a plot:

   1. Introduction- the characters, setting, and necessary background information are introduced

   2. Rising action- the story becomes more complex and the conflict is introduced

      The types of conflict are *man vs. man, man vs. self, man vs. nature, man vs. society,* and *man vs. fate.*

   3. Climax- the height of the conflict and turning point of the story

   4. Falling action- the conflict begins to resolve itself

   5. Resolution- the conflict is resolved and the story concludes

- **Characters-** the people (or sometimes animals or objects) who participate in a story

   The two main types of characters are the **protagonist** (the main character or hero) and the **antagonist** (the character that works against the protagonist).

- **Point of View-** the perspective from which the narration takes place; who is telling the story

   o Main Types of Narrators:

   1. First person- ones of the characters tells the story from his or her own perspective; uses "I"

   2. Third person- the story is told by an outside voice who is not one of the characters

   3. Omniscient- a third person narrator who knows everything about all of the characters, including their inner thoughts and feelings.

   4. Limited omniscient- a third person narrator who only knows the inner thoughts and feelings of one specific character

As students learn to write, it is important for them to learn to write according to a clear process in order to ensure that their writing is given thought and quality. Throughout the writing process, peer editing can be a valuable tool to help students evaluate and revise their work.

The Five Stages of the Writing Process

1. **Prewriting-** brainstorm ideas for writing

2. **Rough Draft-** write down all of the ideas in an organized way

3. **Revise-** reread the rough draft and make changes to how the information is presented and organized; make sure tone, purpose, and audience are clear; add or delete content as needed

4. **Edit-** make changes to spelling, grammar, and other mechanics

5. **Publish-** create the final copy

Writing can take on many forms and be organized in many ways. Structures of writing are devices that help the writing to accomplish its purpose. Some examples of writing structures are:

- **Description**- a writing mode for creating a mental picture of someone or something

- **Definition**- provides a statement of the exact meaning of something

- **Argument**- presents a case in favor of a particular point of view or opinion

- **Examples**- provide evidence to clarify an idea, add details, or to give support to an argument

The organization of a piece can help the writing to fulfill its purpose by conveying meaning in the most effective manner.

Term	Definition
Descriptive	Provides a detailed description of someone or something
Comparison/Contrast	Examines the similarities and differences between two or more things
Cause and Effect	Presents causal relationships between a particular event or idea and those that follow it
Persuasive	Aims to convince the reader of a point of view; will include arguments and supporting evidence
Problem-Solution	Presents a problem, suggest and explains a possible solution, and discusses the potential effects of the solution
Sequential	Presents events in chronological order or presents a set of ordered steps

There are many resources available to teachers in reading and language arts. In addition to traditional print materials, multimedia resources can be used to enhance literacy learning. Teachers should become familiar with the resources available in their schools and communities and integrate them into classroom learning. Sources of information fall under two major categories—primary and secondary sources.

Primary sources are original sources that give a first-hand account of an event by someone who participated in it or observed it at the time that it was happening. Some examples of primary sources are diaries/journals, letters, interviews, and surveys.

Secondary sources are created later by people who did not experience events first-hand. They draw on primary sources as their own source material and present their collected research to the reader. Some examples are research articles, books, and encyclopedias.

When evaluating sources, teachers and students should check for:

- Reliability
- Bias
- Accuracy
- Up to date information

Aspects of Speaking

When speaking, the speaker must take into consideration several aspects of the speaking process. Just like writing, speaking involves purpose, audience, and tone; however, since speaking is a live process rather than something that will be read later, and since the speaker will usually be visible to the audience, other special considerations must come into play. A speaker should make these considerations:

- **Purpose**- Why are you speaking? What do you hope to accomplish?

- **Tone**- What feeling should this have? Funny? Serious?

- **Audience**- Who are you speaking to? What are they like? What are their wants and needs?

- **Occasion**- When and where is this taking place? Is what you are saying appropriate in this setting?

- **Speaker**- How should you present yourself? What preparations should you make?

Listening is more than just hearing words. To listen, understand, and make meaning from spoken words requires active listening. There are several ways to be an effective listener:

- Focusing on the speaker
- Following directions
- Responding to questions appropriately
- Paying attention to non-verbal communication

Aspects of Viewing

Viewing various media requires its own skill set. This includes:

- Interpreting images- finding meaning in visual cues

- Evaluating media techniques- identifying the methods used to create the media and present its message and assess their effectiveness

- Understanding the message- deriving the purpose of the media and the overall idea it is trying to convey

Speaking, listening, and viewing play an important role in language acquisition for second-language learners. Mastery of a language requires the ability to read, write, and speak in the language, and listening and viewing can help to promote the development of those other skills.

For second-language learners, especially in the early stages, frequent opportunities for listening and viewing are essential. Listening enables learners to hear the language aloud and begin to pick up its pronunciation and rhythms. Tone and context are also often easier to detect in spoken language than in written language, which can help the listener to understand more of what is being said. Listening is also essential for learning conversational English, which can be different than conventional written English.

Viewing is also important for second-language learners. Visual aids are tremendously helpful for students trying to learn new vocabulary. It helps them to remember words and creates a link between a written or spoken word and something concrete.

Speaking is often one of the most difficult tasks in learning a second language. Often, learners are able to understand far more language than they are able to correctly produce. Providing ample opportunities for speaking practice in a non-threatening environment is important for their language development.

Mathematics

Knowledge of mathematics is foundational for student success. Students develop skills in mathematical problem solving that transfer to many real world applications and career fields.

Test Structure

The Mathematics subtest consists of 40 multiple choice questions and last for 50 minutes. Within Mathematics, there are two major subcategories with which you must be familiar:

A. Number, Operations, and Algebraic Thinking (65% of Mathematics content)

B. Geometry, Measurement, Data, and Interpretation (35% of Mathematics content)

Each subcategory is divided into standards that state the skills you must be able to demonstrate on the exam.

Number, Operations, and Algebraic Thinking

This portion of the test covers the development of early mathematical knowledge, number theory, the four major operations, and basic algebraic concepts which will lay the foundation for students' future mathematical learning.

Standards Addressed:

A. Number and Operations

1. Prenumeration Concepts
2. Basic Number Systems
3. The Four Basic Operations and Their Properties
4. Basic Concepts of Number Theory

B. Algebraic Thinking

1. Problem-Solving Strategies
2. Numerical Patterns and Mathematical Investigations
3. Basic Algebraic Methods and Representations
4. The Associative, Commutative, and Distributive Properties
5. Additive and Multiplicative Inverses
6. Special Properties of Zero and One
7. Equations and Inequalities
8. Appropriate Allocation of Formulas

Number and Operations

Prenumeration Concepts

Long before they have a math class, young children begin to formulate math-related reasoning. These early ideas are known as **prenumeration concepts**. One such concept is the **meaning of number**. Children learn that numbers refer to quantities of something. Once they understand this, they can begin to count.

Informal counting is one of the first mathematical procedures a child learns. Once kids learn their numbers in sequence, they can begin to associate those numbers with objects and they will begin to point and count at the same time. Young children can also begin to see **patterns** among objects. Recognizing groupings as patterns will eventually develop into higher level mathematical skills as students learn to recognize patterns in numbers and in geometry.

Another early concept is that of **relative magnitude**. This is the ability to make comparisons and determine whether one number is larger or smaller than another.

There are several basic categories of numbers.

- **Natural numbers** are those numbers we typically use to count (1, 2, 3...)

- **Whole numbers** are the natural numbers and zero (0, 1, 2, 3...)

- **Integers** are whole numbers and their corresponding negatives (0.. -3, -2, -1, 0, 1, 2, 3...)

- **Fractions** are portions of integers, expressed with a numerator and a denominator

  (¼, ½, etc.)

- **Decimals** are portions of integers, expressed as numbers following a decimal point

  (0.5, 0.67, etc.)

- **Even numbers** are integers divisible by two (...-6, -4, -2, 2, 4, 6...)

- **Odd numbers** are integers not divisible by two(... -7, -5, -3, 3, 5, 7...)

- **Rational numbers** are all integers and fractions

- **Irrational numbers** are any numbers that cannot be expressed as fractions, such as an infinite, non-repeating decimal

The four basic operations—addition, subtraction, multiplication, and division—serve as the basis for all mathematical processes.

Addition

Addition is bringing two or more numbers (or objects) together to make a new total called a **sum**. A common method used in addition is regrouping by carrying. When adding vertically, add each place value individually, starting on the right and moving left. If any single place value sums to a number greater than 10, keep the value over 10 in that place value and carry the tens place to the next column to be added into that place value.

Example

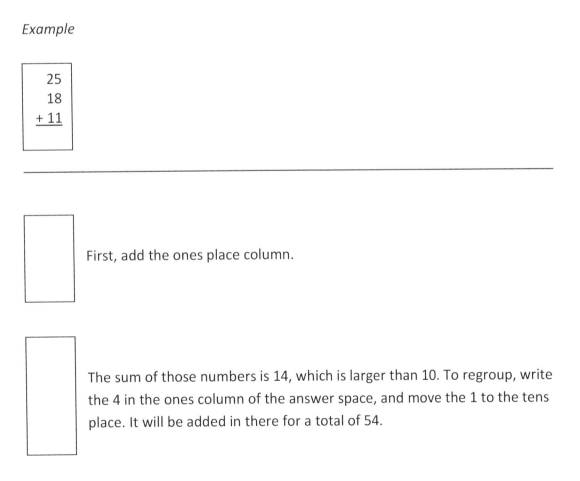

First, add the ones place column.

The sum of those numbers is 14, which is larger than 10. To regroup, write the 4 in the ones column of the answer space, and move the 1 to the tens place. It will be added in there for a total of 54.

Subtraction

Subtraction is taking numbers (or objects) away from a group to create a new total, called a **difference**. A common method used in subtraction is regrouping by borrowing. When subtracting vertically, subtract each place value individually, moving from right to left. If ever the top number (the one you are subtracting *from*) is smaller than the bottom number (the one being subtracted), you will need to borrow. To borrow, add 10 to the digit you were trying to subtract from, then subtract 1 from the next place to the left to compensate.

Example

```
┌───────┐
│       │
│       │
│       │
└───────┘
```

```
┌───────┐
│       │   Start with the ones column.
│       │
│       │
└───────┘
```

```
┌───────┐
│   12  │
│   6̶2̶  │   Notice that the 2 is not large enough to subtract the 7 from it. This
│ - 17  │   means we will need to borrow.
│    5  │
└───────┘
```

```
┌───────┐
│  5 12 │
│   6̶2̶  │   Borrow from the tens column by subtracting 1 from the top number,
│ - 17  │   making the 6 into a 5. Then subtract the tens column. The answer is 45.
│   45  │
└───────┘
```

Multiplication

Multiplication is adding a number to itself a certain number of times. It is ultimately a shortcut to repeated addition. Multiplication quantifies equal groups of things.

The two numbers in a multiplication problem are called the multiplicand and the multiplier. The answer is called the **product**. The typical process for multiplication involves multiplying the multiplicand by each digit of the multiplier, then adding the results to get the product.

Example

```
  42
x 13
```

```
  42
x 13
 126
```
Start by multiplying the multiplicand (42) by the ones place of the multiplier. 4 x 3 = 12 and 2 x 3 =6

```
  42
x 13
 126
 420
```
Then, multiply 42 by the tens place of the multiplier, using a 0 to hold the place value in the ones.

2 x 1 = 2 and 4 x 1 = 4

```
   42
 x 13
  126
+420
  546
```
Finally, add these results to get the final product of 546.

Division

Division is splitting a number into equal groups. The number being divided is the **dividend**, the number it is divided by is the **divisor**, and the answer is the **quotient**.

In division, dividing moves in place values from left to right. Any leftovers that do not divide evenly into the dividend become either a remainder, fraction, or decimal.

Example

$$5\overline{)257}$$

$$\begin{array}{r} 5 \\ 5\overline{)257} \end{array}$$

In this example, 257 is the dividend and 5 is the divisor. Move from left to right in the place values of the dividend. 5 cannot divide into 2.

$$\begin{array}{r} 5 \\ 5\overline{)257} \end{array}$$

Expand to the right and look at the first two digits, 25.

5 *does* divide evenly into 25 (5 times).

$$\begin{array}{r} 51 \text{ R2} \\ 5\overline{)257} \\ -5 \\ 2 \end{array}$$

Now, move to the right again. 5 goes into 7 with a remainder of 2. To divide without remainders, you would add on decimal places until the division comes out evenly. In this case, the result would be 51.4

Note: There are many methods for division other than the long division shown, but the basic elements are still the same.

Order of Operations

When an equation has more than one of these operations in it, the operations must be performed in a certain order. The order can be remembered with the acronym PEMDAS, which stands for:

- **Parentheses**- Complete any operations enclosed within parentheses first. If more than one operation is inside the parentheses, perform the operations within the parentheses in PEMDAS order, then proceed with the operations outside the parentheses.

- **Exponents**- Deal with any exponents next.

- **Multiplication/Division**- Multiplication and division can be done in the same step as one another.

- **Addition/Subtraction**- Addition and subtraction can be done in the same step as one another.

Number theory is the study of numbers and their relationships with one another. Several concepts in number theory are foundational to mathematics at the elementary level and beyond.

Place Value

Place value is a way of organizing numbers based on groupings of ten. The place value in which a digit lays conveys how many groups of ten (or one hundred, or one thousand, etc.) it represents. Place value is also used in decimals.

Whole Numbers						
Millions	Hundred Thousands	Ten Thousands	Thousands	Hundreds	Tens	Units
1,000,000	100,000	10,000	1,000	100	10	1
2,478,390	2,**4**78,390	2,4**7**8,390	2,47**8**,390	2,478,**3**90	2,478,3**9**0	2,478,39**0**

Decimals					
Tenths	Hundredths	Thousandths	Ten Thousandths	Hundred Thousandths	Millionths
.1	.01	.001	.0001	.00001	.000001
.**2**37894	.2**3**7894	.23**7**894	.237**8**94	.2378**9**4	.23789**4**

Factors and Multiples

Factors are whole numbers that are multiplied together to get a product.

- Example: The factors of 16 are 1, 2, 4, 8, and 16.

The processing of breaking a number down into its factors is called **factoring**.

Whole numbers can be classified by how many factors they have as either being prime or composite numbers.

- **Prime numbers** are those numbers (other than zero and one) that have only two factors—themselves and 1

  2, 3, 5, 7, 11...

- **Composite numbers** are any positive integers that are not prime, meaning they have more than two factors

  4, 6, 8, 9, 10...

When comparing the factors of two numbers, the largest factor that they have in common in called the **Greatest Common Factor (GCF)**.

Example:

- Factors of 20: 1, 2, **4**, 5, 10, 20
- Factors of 24: 1, 2, 3, **4**, 6, 8, 12, 24

  GCF: 4

Multiples are the result of multiplying a number by whole numbers.

Example:

- The multiples of 4 are 4, 8, 12, 16, 20, 24...

When comparing the multiples of two numbers, the smallest multiple that they have in common is called the **Least Common Multiple (LCM)**.

Example:

- Multiples of 3: 3, 6, 9, 12, **15**, 18, 21...

- Multiples of 5: 5, 10, **15**, 20, 25, 30...

  LCM: 15

Ratios

A **ratio** is a way to compare two numbers.

Example: If a parent has one son and three daughters, the ratio of sons to daughters would be one to three.

A ratio can be expressed in words, as a fraction, or as two numbers separated by a colon. The ratio "one to three" is the same as "$\frac{1}{3}$" is the same as "1:3."

Proportions

A **proportion** is two ratios set equal to each other. Proportions are often expressed as two fractions with an equals sign between them.

Example: $\frac{1}{3} = \frac{2}{6}$

Proportions that include an unknown can be solved by cross-multiplying.

Example: The ratio of cats to dogs in a pet is 3 to 2. If there are 12 cats, how many dogs are there?

$$\frac{3}{2} = \frac{12}{x}$$

$3x = 12 \times 2$

$3x = 24$

$x = 8$

There are 8 dogs in the pet store.

Percents

Percents convey a ratio out of 100. Percents are represented with a percentage symbol (%). The percentage formula is:

$$\frac{\%}{100} = \frac{part}{whole}$$

It is solved by cross-multiplying.

Algebraic Thinking

Problem Solving Strategies

There are many different methods for solving mathematical problems. No single method will be the most effective for every student on every problem. Some of the strategies students will employ include:

- Modeling

- Estimation

- Using algorithms

- Mental math

- Looking for patterns

- Calculator use

When problem-solving, it is important for students to be able to recognize the reasonableness of results. When they find a solution, they should check to see if their answer makes sense—if the number they have arrived at seems reasonable based on the parameters of the problem. This is a means of self-check.

Numerical Patterns

Some mathematical investigations may require students to make, describe, and/or explore **numerical patterns**. Numerical patterns are sets of numbers that follow a rule that governs the relationship between the numbers and dictates what number will come next in the set. Numerical patterns require students to analyze a set of numbers, discover the relationship between them, and articulate the pattern as a general rule that will work to the nth term in the series. Some examples of common number patterns are:

Pattern Name	Description	Example
Arithmetic Sequence	The same value is added each time	1, 5, 9, 13, 17, 21... (add 4 each time)
Geometric Sequence	The same value is multiplied each time	1, 3, 9, 27, 81... (multiply by 3 each time)
Squares	Square each number (n^2)	1, 4, 9, 16, 25...
Cubes	Cube each number (n^3)	1, 8, 27, 64, 125...
Fibonacci Sequence	Each number is the sum of the two numbers before it	0, 1, 1, 2, 3, 5, 8, 13, 21...
Triangular Sequence	Each number adds what would be another row to a triangle of dots $x_n = n(n+1)/2$ A numerical example of a triangular sequence:	 1, 3, 6, 10, 15, 21, 28, 36...

Mathematical investigations are problems which ask students to formulate their own conjectures, test those conjectures, modify them if need be, and draw conclusions. Engaging in mathematical investigations requires students to employ critical thinking skills, to hypothesize, to collect data, to synthesize information, and to analyze and evaluate.

Solving algebraic equations requires knowledge of such concepts as representation, variables, factorization, and arithmetic operations. In order to solve algebraic problems, students will need to be comfortable with the vocabulary association with the arithmetic operations. This is especially important in word problems where students will need to deduce the operation necessary to solve without being able to see the symbol for the operation.

Addition	Subtraction	Multiplication	Division
Add	Subtract	Multiply	Divide
Sum	Difference	Product	Quotient
More than	Less than	Total	Distribute
Plus	Minus	Times	Per
In addition	Diminished		
Increased	Decreased		
All together	Remove		
Total	Take away		
And	Deduct		

Basic operations have special properties that govern how they work and can make them easier to solve.

Property	Applies To	Description	Example
Commutative Property	Addition and Multiplication	The order of the numbers being added or multiplied does not affect final result	$1 + 3 = 3 + 1$ $2 \times 5 = 5 \times 2$
Distributive Property	Multiplication	$a(b + c) = ab + ac$ Multiplication in front of parenthesis can be distributed to each term within the parentheses.	$2(3+1) =$ $2 \times 3 + 2 \times 1 =$ $6 + 2 =$ 8 This yields the same result as $2(3+1) =$ $2(4) =$ 8
Associative Property	Addition and Multiplication	If the operations are all the same (all addition or all multiplication) the terms can be regrouped by moving the parentheses. $(a + b) + c = a + (b + c)$ $a(bc) = (ab)c$	Addition: $(1 + 2) + 3 = 3 + 3 = 6$ $1 + (2 + 3) = 1 + 5 = 6$ Multiplication: $3(4y) = 12y$ $(3 \times 4)y = 12y$

An **additive inverse** of a number is its equal opposite such that when the two are added together, they will equal 0.

Example

Number	Additive Inverse
1	-1
-25	25
x	-x

The **multiplicative inverse** of a number is the reciprocal of the number such that when the two are multiplied, they equal 1.

Example

Number	Multiplicative Inverse
5	1/5
1/2	2
x	1/x

Absolute Value

A related concept is that of **absolute value**, a number's distance from 0. Absolute value is always positive. If the number is greater than 0, it is its own absolute value. If negative, its additive inverse (the positive equivalent of itself) is its absolute value.

Example

Number	Absolute Value
5	5
-10	10
x	x
-x	x

Zero and one have their own special properties that no other numbers possess.

Properties of Zero

- *Addition property of zero-* Adding 0 to a number does not change the number's value.

  $x + 0 = x$

- *Multiplication property of zero-* Any number multiplied by 0 equals 0

  $0\,x = 0$

- *Additive inverse-* The sum of any number and its additive inverse is 0

  $x + -x = 0$

- *Powers of zero-* 0 raised to any power equals 0

  $0^x = 0$

- *Zero as a dividend-* Dividing 0 by any number results in a quotient of 0

  $0 \div x = 0$

- *Division by zero-* Dividing any number by 0 results in a quotient that is undefined

  $x \div 0 = \text{undefined}$

Properties of One

- *Multiplication property of one-* Multiplying a number by 1 does not change the number's value.

  $1\,x = x$

- *Multiplicative inverse-* The product of any number and its multiplicative inverse is 1

  $x\left(\frac{1}{x}\right) = 1$

- *Powers of one-* 1 raised to any power equals 1

  $1^x = 1$

- *Quotient of one-* Any number (other than 0) divided by itself equals 1

  $x \div x = 1$

Equations can be classified either as equalities or inequalities. Each has its own properties and rules for operations.

Equalities

An **equality** is an equation where both sides are equal and are separated by an equals sign (=). There are several properties of equalities:

- Reflexive property- Every number is equal to itself.

  $x = x$

- Symmetric property- If a number is equal to another number, then the converse is also true.

  If $x = y$ then $y = x$.

- Transitive property- If number a is equal to number b, and number b is equal to number c, then number a is also equal to number c.

  If $x = y$ and $y = z$, then $x = z$.

- Substitution property- If two numbers are equal to one another, they are interchangeable.

  If $x = y$, then $x + z = y + z$

- Property of addition, subtraction, multiplication, and division- If two numbers are equal, they will remain equal if the same number is added to or subtracted from them, or if they are multiplied or divided by the same number.

  If $x = y$, then $x + z = y + z$

  If $x = y$, then $x - z = y - z$

  If $x = y$, then $xz = yz$

  If $x = y$, then $x/z = y/z$

Inequalities

An **inequality** is an equation where the two sides are not necessarily equal. The two sides of the equation are separated by one of the following symbols:

- $<$ *less than*
- $>$ *greater than*
- $\leq$ *less than or equal to*
- $\geq$ *greater than or equal to*

With inequalities, operations performed to one side must be performed to the other. When adding or subtracting the same value from both sides, or when multiplying or dividing by a positive number on both sides, the inequality sign does not change. When multiplying or dividing by a negative number, the inequality sign is reversed.

Formulas are standard equations with variables that follow specific rules and are used to solve specific types of problems. Below are several examples of fundamental algebraic formulas.

- *Difference of two perfect squares*

$$a^2 - b^2 = (a + b)(a - b)$$

- *Distance formula*- used to measure the distance between two points on a coordinate plane

$$d = \sqrt{(x_2 - x_1)^2 + (y_2 - y_1)^2}$$

- *Laws of exponents*

Types of Laws	Law	Example
Product Rules	$a^n \cdot a^m = a^{n+m}$	$2^2 \cdot 2^3 = 2^{2+3} = 32$
	$a^n \cdot b^n = (a \cdot b)^n$	$2^2 \cdot 3^2 = (2 \cdot 3)^2 = 36$
Quotient Rules	$a^n / a^m = a^{n-m}$	$2^5 / 2^3 = 2^{5-3} = 4$
	$a^n / b^n = (a / b)^n$	$4^3 / 2^3 = (4/2)^3 = 8$
Power Rules	$(b^n)^m = b^{n \cdot m}$	$(2^3)^4 = 2^{3 \cdot 4} = 4096$
	$^m\sqrt{(b^n)} = b^{n/m}$	$^2\sqrt{(2^4)} = 2^{4/2} = 4$
Negative Exponents	$b^{-n} = 1 / b^n$	$2^{-3} = 1/2^3 = 0.125$
Zero Rules	$b^0 = 1$	$9^0 = 1$
	$0^n = 0$, for $n>0$	$0^3 = 0$
One Rules	$b^1 = b$	$7^1 = 7$
	$1^n = 1$	$1^4 = 1$

- *Midpoint formula*- used to find the midpoint between two points on a coordinate plane

$$\left(\frac{(x_2 + x_1)}{2}, \frac{(y_2 + y_1)}{2} \right)$$

- *Pythagorean theorem*- used to find a missing length of a right triangle

$$a^2 + b^2 = c^2$$

- *Quadratic formula*- a method of solving a quadratic equation ($ax^2 + bx + c = 0$)

  $$x = \frac{-b \pm \sqrt{b^2 - 4ac}}{2a}$$

- *Slope formula*- used to find the slope of a line on a coordinate plane

  $$m = \frac{y_2 - y_1}{x_2 - x_1}$$

- *Slope intercept formula*- the equation of a straight line

  $y = mx + b$ where *m* is the slope and *b* is the y-intercept

Geometry, Measurement, Data, and Interpretation

At the elementary level, students learn foundational geometric concepts as well as procedures for measuring with different unit systems and interpreting measurement data.

Standards Addressed:

A. Geometry

1. Properties and Relationships of 2D and 3D Figures
2. Transformations, Geometric Models and Nets

B. Measurement, Data, and Interpretation

1. Nonstandard, Customary, and Metric Units of Measurement
2. Visual Displays of Quantitative Data
3. Simple Probability and Intuitive Concepts of Chance
4. Fundamental Counting Techniques
5. Basic Descriptive Statistics

Geometry

Properties and Relationships of 2D and 3D Figures

Points

A **point** is an exact location on a plane surface.

.P

On a coordinate plane, a point is identified by a set of coordinates, giving the x and y values of the point's location on the coordinate plane.

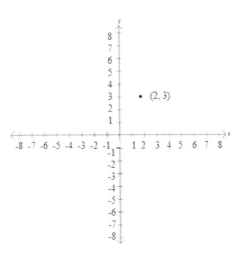

73

Lines, Line Segments, and Rays

A **line** is an object that is straight, thin, and infinitely long. It has arrows on both ends to show that it goes on forever in both directions.

Two special types of lines are parallel lines and perpendicular lines. **Parallel lines** are always equally spaced so that they never intersect each other.

Perpendicular lines intersect at a 90º angle.

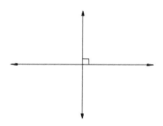

A **line segment** is a portion of a line that has two endpoints, which give it a definite length.

A **ray** has only one endpoint and is infinite in the other direction.

Angles

An **angle** is the space formed by two rays that meet at a common endpoint. Angles are measured in degrees.

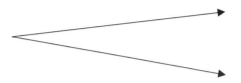

Angle Type	Definition	Example
Acute	The angle measures less than 90º	
Right	The angle measures exactly 90º	
Obtuse	The angle measures between 90º and 180º	
Straight	The angle measures exactly 180º	
Reflex	The angle measures greater than 180º	

Angles can also be described by their relationships to one another.

- **Complimentary angles** are those whose measures add up to 90º.

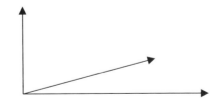

- **Supplementary angles** are those whose measures add up to 180º.

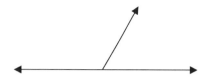

Two-Dimensional Shapes

A two-dimensional closed figure can be classified either as a polygon or a non-polygon. A **polygon** is a closed two-dimensional figure whose sides are all straight, non-overlapping line segments. A polygon is said to be **regular** if all of its sides and angles are equal and irregular if they are not. **Non-polygons** do not have sides that are all straight line segments and include such shapes as ellipses and circles. Polygons can be classified by the number of sides they have.

Name	Number of Sides
Triangle	3
Quadrilateral	4
Pentagon	5
Hexagon	6
Heptagon	7
Octagon	8
Nonagon	9
Decagon	10

Some of these categories of polygons can also be further broken down into subcategories. The most common ones elementary students will encounter are triangles and quadrilaterals. Triangles can be classified either by the types of angles they have or the length of their sides.

Triangles Classified by Angles		
Type of Triangles	**Description**	**Example**
Acute	All three angles are acute (measure less than 90º)	
Right	One angle is right (measures exactly 90º)	
Obtuse	One angle is obtuse (measures between 90º and 180º)	

Triangles Classified by Sides		
Type of Triangles	**Description**	**Example**
Equilateral	All three sides are equal in length	
Isosceles	Two sides are equal in length	
Scalene	No sides are equal in length	

Quadrilaterals can be divided into several subcategories based on characteristics such as angles, parallelism, and side length.

Quadrilateral- *four sides*	
Trapezoid- *one pair of parallel sides*	**Parallelogram-** *two pairs of equal parallel sides*

Rectangle- *four right angles*	Rhombus-- *four equal sides*
Square - *four right angles and four equal sides*	

The measure of the distance around a polygon is called the **perimeter**. The perimeter is found by adding up the lengths of all of the sides of a figure.

The distance around the outside of a circle is called the **circumference.** The circumference is found with the formula $C = \pi d$ or $C = 2\pi r$ where r is the radius and d is the diameter.

The measure of the space inside a two-dimensional figure is called the **area**.

Common Area Formulas	
Triangle	$A = \frac{1}{2} bh$
Parallelogram	$A = bh$
Rectangle	$A = lw$
Square	$A = s^2$
Circle	$A = \pi r^2$

Three-Dimensional Shapes

A three-dimensional shape is a solid figure. There are several categories of solid figures, some of which are listed in the following chart:

Shape	Description	Example
Sphere	Round three-dimensional figure, like a ball	
Pyramid	Triangular of square base, with all other sides triangular that come together at a single point	
Rectangular prism	Six rectangular faces	
Cylinder	Two circular bases	
Cone	One circular base	
Cube	Six square faces	

The measure of the **surface area** of a prism is found by adding up the areas of each of the faces. The measure of the space inside a three-dimensional object (its capacity) is called **volume**.

- Volume of a prism:

  $V = bh$ where b is the area of the base of the prism

- Volume of a pyramid or cone:

  $V = \frac{1}{3}bh$ where b is the area of the base of the object

- Volume of a sphere:

  $V = \frac{4}{3}\pi r^3$

Transformations

Transformations are a way of manipulating geometric figures by changing their positions on a coordinate plane. There are three basic types of transformations.

Name of Transformation	Description	Example
Reflection (Flip)	The transformed shape is a mirror image of the original	
Rotation (Turn)	The shape is turned on a point	
Translation (Slide)	The shape is shifted to another area on the plane but maintains its original orientation	

Geometric Models and Nets

A **geometric model** can be constructed to show the shape of an object in geometric terms.

Geometric nets are two-dimensional figures that represent the faces of a three-dimensional shape. It's as if the three-dimensional figure has been cut apart along the edges and made to lay flat. Only certain three-dimensional figures can be made into geometric nets. Two of the most common examples are cubes and tetrahedrons (pyramids with a triangular base).

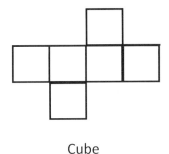

Cube

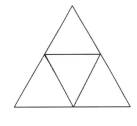

Tetrahedron

Measurement, Data, and Interpretation

Nonstandard, Customary and Metric Units of Measurement

Students will learn to understand measurement concepts using different sets of units. The three main types of units students will encounter are nonstandard, customary, and metric units.

Nonstandard Measurement

Nonstandard measurement is how elementary students first learn to measure. The use of nonstandard units often involves measuring using small objects such as paper clips.

Customary Measurement

Customary measurement is the primary system of measurement used in the United States. There are customary units to measure length, weight, volume, temperature, and time.

Length is measured in inches, feet, yards, and miles.

- 12 inches (in. or ") = 1 foot (ft. or ')

- 36 inches = 3 feet = 1 yard (yd.)

- 5,280 feet = 1,760 yards = 1 mile (mi.)

Weight is measured in ounces, pounds, and tons.

- 16 ounces (oz.) = 1 pound (lb.)

- 1,000 pounds = 1 ton (T.)

Volume is measured in fluid ounces, cups, pints, quarts, and gallons.

- 8 fluid ounces (fl. oz.) = 1 cup (c.)

- 16 fluid ounces = 2 cups = 1 pint (pt.)

- 4 cups = 2 pints = 1 quart (qt.)

- 8 pints = 4 quarts = 1 gallon (gal.)

Temperature is measured in degrees Fahrenheit (°F).

Time is measured in seconds, minutes, and hours.

- 60 seconds (sec.) = 1 minute (min.)

- 60 minutes = 1 hour (hr.)

Metric Measurement

The metric system of measurement is used in most of the world. It is based on units that are multiples of ten. No matter what is being measured, the units have prefixes which tell you the size of the unit relative to the others of its type.

The basic unit for each form of measurement is:

- Length- meter

- Mass- gram

- Volume- liter

Adding one of the prefixes in the chart below changes the value.

Kilo-	Hecto-	Deka-	Unit	Deci-	Centi-	Milli-
.001	.01	.1	1	10	100	1000

For example, this means that 1 gram is equal to 1000 milligrams. To convert between units in the metric system, simply use this chart to determine how many places to move the decimal.

The metric system has two scales for measuring temperature—Celsius (°C) and Kelvin (K).

Quantitative information can be displayed visually with the use of charts and graphs. There are several common types of charts and graphs with which elementary students should be familiar.

Pictographs

Pictographs use pictures or symbols to represent pieces of data. A symbol may represent one item or a key may indicate that each symbol represents more than one item. Quantities of each item are obtained by counting the symbols.

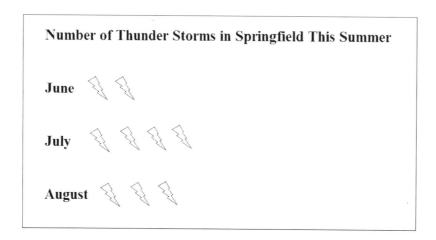

Bar Graphs

Bar graphs use bars to represent quantities. The quantity represented by each bar is obtained by reading the height of the bar.

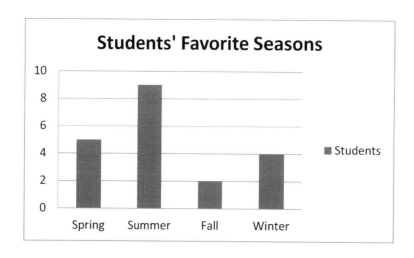

Pie Graphs

Pie graphs are used to show information in relation to a whole. The circle represents a whole and is divided into segments to represent the portions. The portions are usually shown in percentages.

Line Graphs

Line graphs use lines to connect data points and are used to show change over time.

Probability is the likelihood of an event occurring. Probability is expressed as a quantifiable relationship between favorable outcomes and possible outcomes. It can be written as a ratio, fraction, decimal, or percent.

A **favorable outcome** is an event someone wants to happen. **Possible outcomes** are all of the events that could happen in a given situation.

Simple probability (P) is the ratio of favorable outcomes (O_f) to possible outcomes (O_p).

$$P_{event} = \frac{O_f}{O_p}$$

- Example 1: *What is the probability of a coin toss landing on heads?*

  When flipping a coin, there are two possible outcomes—heads or tails. The probability of getting heads is 1/2.

- Example 2: *What is the probability of rolling a 5 on a die?*

  When rolling a standard six-sided die, there are six possible outcomes. Rolling a 5 (the favorable outcome) is one of those possibilities. The probability of rolling a 5 is therefore 1/6.

- Example 3: *Using a spinner with equal segments numbered 1-10, what is the probability of a spin landing on an even number?*

  In this case, there are ten possible outcomes—landing on each of the ten segments. The favorable outcome is landing on an even number. In the set of numbers 1-10, there are five even numbers (2, 4, 6, 8, and 10). Any one of these would be a favorable outcome. The probability of landing on a even number is therefore 5/10, which reduces to 1/2.

The Fundamental Counting Principle

The **fundamental counting principle** states that if there are *m* ways to for one thing to happen and *n* ways for another thing to happen, then there are *m* x *n* ways for both to happen.

Example:

If you have 5 shirts and 3 pairs of pants, how many different outfits could you make?

5 x 3 = 15 outfits

These types of problems can also be solved using a visual aid called a **tree diagram**. A tree diagram lists all of the possible combinations of two events. The tree diagram for the example scenario above would look like this:

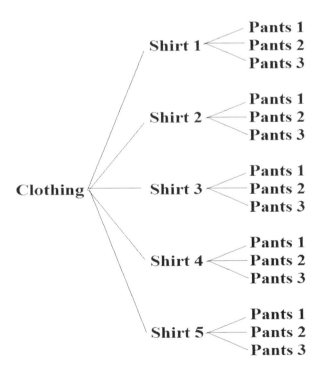

Counting all of the right-most possibilities (those farthest from the "trunk" of the tree) gives the total number of possibilities. In this case, the total is twelve possible outcomes.

Combinations

A **combination** involves choosing items (*r*) out of a group (*n*) in a situation where the order does not matter and there is no repetition.

The formula for a combination is:

$$_nC_r = \frac{n!}{(n-r)!r!}$$

This formula involves the use of **factorials**, represented by the exclamation point (!). A factorial is the product of a number and all of the counting numbers below it.

For example, 4! = 4 x 3 x 2 x 1 = 24

Example: *How many different groups of 3 students can be made from a class of 21?*

$$_nC_r = \frac{n!}{(n-r)!r!}$$

$$_{21}C_3 = \frac{21!}{(21-3)!3!}$$

$$_{21}C_3 = \frac{51090942171709440000}{18!3!}$$

$$_{21}C_3 = \frac{51090942171709440000}{(16402373705728000)(6)}$$

$$_{21}C_3 = \frac{51090942171709440000}{38414242234368000}$$

$$_{21}C_3 = 1{,}330$$

There are 1,330 possible groups.

Permutations

Permutations involve selecting items (*r*) out of a group (*n*) wherein the order *does* matter and there is no repetition. These problems involve arranging items in a certain order.

The formula for a permutation is:

$$_nP_r = \frac{n!}{(n-r)!}$$

Example: *How many different three-digit numbers can be made using only the digits 1, 3, 5, and 7?*

There are 4 digits to choose from and 3 are being selected.

$$_nP_r = \frac{n!}{(n-r)!}$$

$$_4P_3 = \frac{4!}{(4-3)!}$$

$$_4P_3 = \frac{24}{1}$$

$$_4P_3 = 24$$

There are 24 possible three-digit numbers.

Descriptive statistics are used to explain patterns and relationships among sets of data. The basic types of descriptive statistics include mean, median, mode, and range.

Mean

Mean is another word for average. To find the mean of a set of numbers, add the numbers together and divide the sum by how many numbers there are.

Example:

Find the mean of the following set: (12, 15, 18, 20, 21)

$$\frac{12+15+18+20+21}{5} = \frac{86}{5} = 17.2$$

Median

The median of a set of numbers is the number that is in the middle of the set when they are arranged in numerical order. If there are an even number of digits, the median is found by taking the average of the two numbers that are in the center (add them and divide by 2).

Example 1: *Find the median of the following set: (34, 25, 82, 11, 47)*

In order, the set would read 11, 25, 34, 47, 82.

The number in the middle (the median) is 34.

Example 2: *Find the median of the following set: (47, 23, 24, 89, 23, 43)*

In order, the set would read 23, 23, 24, 43, 47, 89.

In the middle are 24 and 43. Take their average to find the median.

$$\frac{24+43}{2} = \frac{67}{2} = 33.5$$

Mode

The mode is the number in a set that appears the most frequently. A set can have one mode, more than one mode, or no mode.

Example: *Find the mode of the following set: (34, 52, 34, 58, 31, 19)*

The number that appears most frequently is 34. 34 is the mode.

Range

The **range** of a set describes the span between the numbers. The range is calculated by subtracting the lowest value in the set from the highest.

Example: *Find the range of the following set: (2, 59, 27)*

The highest number in the set is 59. The lowest number is 2.

59 – 2 = 57

The range is 57.

Social Studies

Social Studies introduces students to topics in history, geography, and social science in an effort to equip them to become informed and contributing members of a democratic society.

Test Structure

The Social Studies subtest consists of 55 multiple choice questions and is 50 minutes long. Within Social Studies, there are three major subcategories with which you must be familiar:

A. United States History, Government, and Citizenship (45% of Social Studies content)

B. Geography, Anthropology, and Sociology (30% of Social Studies content)

C. World History and Economics (25% of Social Studies content)

Each subcategory is divided into standards which state the skills you must be able to demonstrate on the exam.

United States History, Government, and Citizenship

Students should have an understanding of the causes and effects of the major events in the history of the United States, from its colonization to the present day. Students study the government in order to better understand the society in which they live and so that they may become informed, active citizens of the democracy. It is important for students to understand how the government operates, as well as the rights and responsibilities of the nation's citizens.

Standards Addressed:

1. European Exploration/Colonization and U.S. Growth and Expansion

2. The American Revolution and the Founding of the U.S.

3. Major Events and Developments in United States History

4. 20th Century Developments and Transformations

5. Connections Between Causes and Effects of Events

6. The Nature, Purpose, and Forms of Government

7. Key Documents and Speeches in the History of the United States

8. The Rights and Responsibilities of Citizenship in a Democracy

European Exploration

Starting in the 1400s, European powers began to look to expand their influence outward. They sent explorers to find new trade routes and new lands that could be used for their natural resources. During this period, European explorers learned about the existence of the North and South American continents and began to colonize these areas, which were collectively called the New World. Part of this territory would one day become the United States.

The three main motivations for exploration of the New World were:

- Glory- the desire for personal status and to bring prestige to the home country

- God- convert native populations to Christianity

- Gold- get riches for themselves and natural resources, new trade routes, and trading partners for the home country

Students should be familiar with some of the major explorers who navigated the Americas.

Explorer	Nation of Origin	Achievements
John Cabot	Great Britain	Explored the east coast of Canada
Christopher Columbus	Italy, sailed for Spain	"Discovered" North America while looking for a western route to India
Amerigo Vespucci	Italy	The first to realize the Americas were separate continents from Asia; America is named after him
Vasco de Balboa	Spain	First to reach the Pacific by crossing Central America
Juan Ponce de Leon	Spain	First to explore Florida while searching for the Fountain of Youth
Ferdinand Magellan	Spain	First to circumnavigate the globe by sailing around the southern tip of South America
Hernan Cortez	Spain	Conquered Mexico from the Aztecs
Francisco Pizzaro	Spain	Conquered the Incan Empire
Jacques Cartier	France	Explored Canada and claimed it for France
Fernando de Soto	Spain	Discovered the Mississippi River
Francisco Coronado	Spain	Explored the American southwest
Walter Raleigh	Great Britain	Established English colonies in North America
Henry Hudson	Great Britain	Explored northeastern North America and the Arctic
James Cook	Great Britain	Explored the Pacific; discovered Hawaii

The Thirteen Colonies

The British established thirteen colonies along the east coast of what is now the United States. Within the Thirteen Colonies, there were three main regions—New England, Middle Atlantic, and the Southern Colonies. Each area developed its own unique characteristics.

Region	Colonies	Characteristics
New England Colonies	New Hampshire, Massachusetts, Rhode Island, Connecticut	• Rocky soil was poor for farming • Relied on fishing and shipping industries • Most people lived in or near towns • Major city: Boston
Middle Atlantic Colonies	New York, New Jersey, Pennsylvania, Delaware	• Good conditions for farming • The "breadbasket" of the colonies • Fur trade • Major city: Philadelphia
Southern Colonies	Maryland, Virginia, North Carolina, South Carolina, Georgia	• Plantation farming (tobacco, indigo, rice, cotton) • Slavery • More rural population • Major cities: Richmond, Charleston

After the American Revolution, these colonies would become the first thirteen states. They served as the foundation for a nation that would eventually grow to include fifty states across a vast expanse of territory.

The Thirteen Colonies eventually wanted to rule themselves rather than continue to be controlled by Great Britain. This resulted in the American Revolution.

Causes of the American Revolution

When the colonies were first settled, they relied heavily on help from the British. They needed British supplies, British money, the British government to keep order, and the British military for protection. Over time, as the colonies grew more established and stronger, they became more self-sufficient. They no longer relied on the British for everything. They even made their own local governments to make decisions. The less they depended on the British, the more they felt like they didn't need them anymore and that they could govern themselves.

In the late 1700s, the British found themselves in need of money after the costly French and Indian War, so they began to impose many new taxes on the colonists. These included:

- Stamp Act (1765)

- Townshend Acts (1767)

- Tea Act (1773)

- Intolerable Acts (1774)

The colonists did not have representation in the British Parliament, which levied the taxes, so they didn't think it was fair that they should be taxed. After failed attempts at negotiation and compromise, tensions escalated and eventually erupted into war—the American Revolution.

Major Events in the American Revolution

The **American Revolution** began with the **Battle of Lexington and Concord** in 1775. This was soon followed by the **Battle of Bunker Hill**.

The next summer, representatives from the colonies signed a document called the **Declaration of Independence**, which listed the reasons for the rebellion and stated that the United States was to be an independent country. It was signed on July 4, 1776.

Britain was not ready to accept American independence, however, and the war continued. While the British army was more established, better trained, and had larger numbers, the Americans had the advantage of fighting on their own familiar territory and eventually secured aid from the French. The Americans won the war with a final victory at the **Battle of Yorktown** in 1781. The war officially concluded with the signing of the Treaty of Paris in 1783.

Forming a New Nation

The new nation had to create a government for itself. The first system they tried was organized around a document called the **Articles of Confederation**. This made the new government too weak, however, and it ultimately failed.

In 1787, the Articles of Confederation were replaced with a new form of government, outlined in the **U.S. Constitution**. The Constitution set up a federal system with a three-branch national government. Revolutionary War hero George Washington was chosen as the first President of the United States. More details on the Constitution will be explored in the Nature, Purposes, and Forms of Government section.

The United States Expands

Over the course of its history, the United States made several major expansions, enlarging its land from thirteen original states to the current fifty.

The British had holdings in North America other than the Thirteen Colonies. Part of this was in Canada, and remained in British hands following the American Revolution. Some of this territory was adjacent to the Thirteen Colonies and became a part of the new United States. Originally, the Thirteen Colonies turned into the first thirteen states of the United States. The additional territory, which included lands between the Appalachian Mountains and the Mississippi River, was eventually settled. The territories each eventually applied for statehood and became Ohio, Indiana, Illinois, Alabama, Mississippi, Michigan, and Wisconsin.

The next major territorial expansion of the United States occurred in 1803 when President Thomas Jefferson bought the Louisiana Territory from France. The **Louisiana Purchase** doubled the size of the nation, adding what would eventually become Louisiana, Arkansas, Missouri, Iowa, Minnesota, North Dakota, South Dakota, Kansas, Nebraska, Oklahoma, Colorado, Wyoming, and Montana.

This major expansion gave birth to the idea that the United States should one day possess the lands all the way to the Pacific Ocean. The belief that this was the nation's God-given right became known as **Manifest Destiny**. Fueled by this spirit, the nation continued to expand.

The United States purchased Florida from Spain in 1819. In 1845, it annexed Texas, which was at the time an independent republic. The Oregon Territory was acquired in 1846. The **Mexican Cession** of 1848, which followed the Mexican-American War, resulted in the acquisition of the territories that would become California, Nevada, New Mexico, Arizona, and Utah. The **Gadsden Purchase** (1853, from Mexico) completed the territories of Arizona and New Mexico. Alaska was purchased from Russia in 1867 and Hawaii was annexed in 1898.

The Civil War and Reconstruction

The young nation soon became divided over the issue of slavery. States in the South permitted slavery while those in the North did not. The interests of the two regions were relatively balanced in Congress until new states started to be added in the western territories. Pro- and anti-slavery supporters each feared losing power in Congress and fought for the new states to join their side.

Eventually, the conflict escalated and the South seceded (left) the Union, forming the Confederate States of America. The United States, led by President Abraham Lincoln, did not accept the secession and fought the **Civil War** (1861-1865) in order to preserve the unity of the nation. In the end, the North won, the nation was reunited, and slavery was abolished with the passage of the **13th Amendment**.

The period following the Civil War was known as **Reconstruction**. During this period, the government worked to rebuild the South, which had been devastated by the war. Methods used during Reconstruction were controversial and led to continued resentment by many southerners. Following Reconstruction, African Americans, now free from slavery, found themselves subject to legal discrimination in the South, including segregation and voting restrictions. Many migrated to cities in the North.

Industrialization

In the mid-1800s, the United States became part of an international phenomenon known as the Industrial Revolution. During this period, rapid advancements were made in technology that allowed for production to change over from cottage industries to factory systems. This allowed for mass-production of goods.

The impact of the Industrial Revolution was far-reaching. Goods could now be manufactured quickly and cheaply. This led to great economic growth for the United States. Factories provided new jobs for many people, including the nation's large influx of immigrants. All of those factory jobs also drew people into cities, leading to widespread urbanization. It also led to the homogenization of culture as people across the nation were able to access and afford the same goods. Technologies produced during the Industrial Revolution would shape the modern world.

Some negative effects of the Industrial Revolution included hazardous working conditions in factories, poor living conditions in crowded urban areas, and pollution. The Progressive Movement of the early 20th century, led by President Teddy Roosevelt, sought to put in place regulations to help solve some of these problems, including anti-monopoly laws, new economic rules and environmental regulations.

World War I

Though it initially sought neutrality, the United States became involved in World War I (1914-1918) in 1917 due to a combination of factors, including the Germans' use of unrestricted submarine warfare, the sinking of the *Lusitania*, and the Zimmerman Telegram.

The United States joined on the side of the Allied Powers and helped lead them to victory. The war ended with the Treaty of Versailles.

The Interwar Period

Following World War I, the United States once again sought isolation from the rest of the world, not wanting to be dragged into another war. For this reason, it declined to join the newly formed League of Nations.

The 1920s saw a period of economic prosperity for the United States. The decade became known as the **Roaring Twenties**. Economically, it was marked by mass consumerism, buying on credit, and the growth of the power of the stock market. Socially, this was the period when women gained the right to vote, when the automobile became popular, and when jazz music came to be.

The high period of the 1920s came to an abrupt end in 1929, when a massive stock market crash led to the **Great Depression**. A combination of factors, including excess spending, speculation, agricultural overproduction, and buying on margin led to the economic downturn. During the Great Depression, inflation and unemployment were high, banks failed, and families throughout the nation found themselves enduring economic hardship.

President Franklin D. Roosevelt alleviated some of the suffering in the Great Depression with his **New Deal** programs, which gave the government a more active role in the economy. The Great Depression did not come to an end, however, until World War II jumpstarted the economy by providing industrial jobs and demanding a high output of military goods.

World War II

When **World War II** (1939-1945) broke out in Europe, the United States tried to remain neutral. Once again, however, it was eventually pulled into the conflict. The immediate cause of the U.S. entry into World War II was the Japanese bombing of **Pearl Harbor** in 1941.

The United States joined the war on the side of the Allies and fought both in Europe against the Germans and Italians and in Asia against the Japanese. U.S. forces were able to provide necessary reinforcement to Allied troops in Europe, securing the victory on that front. After a drawn out battle in the Pacific, the United States brought the war to a swift end with the dropping of the first **atomic bombs** on the Japanese cities of Hiroshima and Nagasaki.

The war concluded with the Treaty of Paris. The **United Nations** was soon established as an international peacekeeping organization to replace the League of Nations. The United States joined as a prominent member.

The Cold War

Following World War II, Europe was devastated by the conflict, leaving two superpowers left on the world stage—the United States and the Soviet Union. The two nations had competing ideologies (capitalism vs. communism; individualism vs. collectivism) and both wished to spread their ideals to other nations. This led to rivalry. The conflict was greatly intensified by the fact that both sides had nuclear weapons. An attack by either would have had devastating global consequences, so the **Cold War** became decades of competition and threats without direct military conflict.

The two sides fought indirectly in two major **proxy wars**, in which each nation backed a side in a foreign civil war. The **Korean War** (1950-1953) saw communist North Korea, aided by the U.S.S.R., fight to take over South Korea, aided by the United States. The conflict ended in a ceasefire with no changes in boundaries. The **Vietnam War** (1956-1975) saw communist North Vietnam (along with communists in South Vietnam called the Viet Cong), aided by the U.S.S.R., attempt to take over South Vietnam, backed by the United States. The United States eventually withdrew from the long and unpopular war, and the North won, uniting the two territories into the single communist nation of Vietnam. The Cold War came to an end in 1991 when the Soviet Union dissolved due to internal problems.

The Post-Cold War Era

The 1990s were marked by an period of economic growth and prosperity. The decade also saw the rise of the Internet Age, which has revolutionized modern society. The United States was involved in international conflicts during the 1990s, including the Persian Gulf War and Bosnia.

The early twenty-first century has been marked domestically by an economic downturn. In foreign policy, the War on Terror (in response to terrorist attacks on September 11, 2001) has shaped more than a decade of international relations. The United States has fought in long wars in Afghanistan and in Iraq.

Technological advancements were rapid and far-reaching in the twentieth century. The wide array of innovations has changed modern society. Below is just a small sampling of the many developments of the twentieth century that have had a lasting impact.

- Communication technology- radio, television, cellular phones, computers, the internet

- Transportation technology- automobile, airplane, space travel

- Weaponry- nuclear weapons, chemical weapons

It is important for students to understand cause and effect relationships. Such knowledge is essential for drawing meaning from the study of historical events.

Some examples of cause and effect relationships in the history of the United States are listed in the chart below.

Cause	Event	Effect
Taxation without representation	The American Revolution	Independence of the United States
Disputes over slavery and states' rights	The Civil War	The abolition of slavery
Buying on margin, excessive spending, risky investments, agricultural overproduction	The Great Depression	Bank failure, unemployment, inflation

Governments are created to maintain order in a society and for the protection of individuals' lives, liberties, and properties. Governments establish laws in order to protect these things and to prevent conflicts among people.

Forms of Government

Governments throughout history and around the world have taken on many different forms.

Form of Government	Description
Authoritarian	Government maintains strict control over the people
Autocracy	Rule by a single, authoritarian leader
Democracy	Rule by the people (via majority votes)
Direct democracy	The people vote directly on laws
Dictatorship	A single ruler has absolute authority and is unencumbered by a constitution
Monarchy	Government by a single, hereditary ruler
Oligarchy	Rule by a small group of people
Republic	Citizens elect representatives to make laws for them
Theocracy	Rule by a religious group
Totalitarianism	A government that has complete control over all aspects of citizens' lives and employs censorship, coercion, and oppressive means to ensure compliance

The Government of the United States

The United States is considered a democratic republic. The operations of its government are outlined in the **United States Constitution**.

The government of the United States is a **federal system**, which means that power is divided between the national and state governments. Powers allocated to the national government (e.g. the military, warfare, interstate commerce, coining money) are called **delegated powers**. Powers that belong to the states (e.g. professional licensing, intrastate commerce, establishing schools) are called **reserved powers**. Powers that are shared by both the national and state governments (e.g. taxation, making laws, having courts) are called **concurrent powers**. Within each state, there are also local governments that make day-to-day decisions affecting their communities.

At the national level, power is divided between three branches of government. This **separation of powers** ensures that no one person or group has all the power. The branches are the executive, legislative, and judicial branches. Each branch has its own responsibilities, which include **checks and balances** on the other branches.

	Executive Branch	Legislative Branch	Judicial Branch
Who?	President, Vice-President	Congress (House of Representatives and Senate)	Supreme Court
How Chosen	Elected for 4-year terms	House: elected for 2-year terms Senate: elected for 6-year terms	Appointed by the President and approved by Congress; serve for life
Main Duty	Enforce the laws	Make the laws	Interpret the laws
Checks on Other Branches	• Appoints Supreme Court nominees • Can veto laws	• Must approve Supreme Court nominees • Can override presidential veto • can impeach president of Supreme Court justices	• Can declare laws or presidential actions unconstitutional

The Constitution was intended to be flexible, allowing it to change as necessary with the times. This is why it includes a process for adding **amendments**, or changes, to the document. Currently, there are twenty-seven amendments. The first ten amendments are collectively known as the **Bill of Rights** and they outline citizens' basic rights and freedoms.

The Bill of Rights	
1st Amendment	Freedoms of speech, religion, press, assembly, and petition
2nd Amendment	Right to bear arms
3rd Amendment	Protection against quartering of soldiers
4th Amendment	Protection against illegal search and seizure
5th Amendment	Right to due process; protection against self-incrimination and double jeopardy
6th Amendment	Rights to a speedy trial by jury, to hear accusations and confront the accuser, to witnesses, and to counsel
7th Amendment	Right to trial by jury in civil cases
8th Amendment	Protection against cruel and unusual punishment
9th Amendment	Protects rights not enumerated in the Constitution
10th Amendment	Limits the powers of the federal government to those designated in the Constitution

Key Documents and Speeches in U.S. History

Throughout the history of the United States, there have been important documents and speeches that have shaped political life in this nation.

Document/Speech	Written/Delivered By	When	Description
Mayflower Compact	Pilgrims on the Mayflower	1620	Set up a temporary government for the Pilgrims at Plymouth Colony
Common Sense	Thomas Paine	1775	Pamphlet written to convince people to support the American Revolution
Declaration of Independence	Second Continental Congress; main author- Thomas Jefferson	1776	Stated reasons for the American Revolution and asserted the nation's independence from Great Britain
Articles of Confederation	Second Continental Congress	1781	Set up the first government for the newly independent United States
Federalist Papers	James Madison, Alexander Hamilton, John Jay	1787	Papers written to convince people to ratify the Constitution
U.S. Constitution	Constitutional Convention	1787	Document that set up the current system of U.S. government
Farewell Address	George Washington	1796	Departing President Washington advised the young nation against political factions and entangling foreign alliances
Gettysburg Address	Abraham Lincoln	1863	Speech given by President Lincoln in the midst of the Civil War as a memorial to those who died at the Battle of Gettysburg and to motivate the North to keep fighting to preserve the Union and to end slavery
Emancipation Proclamation	Abraham Lincoln	1865	Declared an end to slavery in the Confederate states

The Rights and Responsibilities of Citizenship in a Democracy

A democratic system relies on having citizens who are active participants. Citizens have certain rights and responsibilities to their nation.

In a democracy, the power of the government is limited and the leaders are ultimately responsible to the people. Citizens of the United States aged eighteen and older have the right to vote, which enables them to choose leaders who will represent their interests in the government. Citizens have a responsibility to stay knowledgeable about political issues and to vote according to their conscience to choose the best leaders for the nation.

Citizens can also practice good citizenship by staying politically active, well-informed, and involved in community service and activities. Responsible citizens understand that it takes a group of people working together for a community to function effectively.

Geography, anthropology, and sociology are foundational components of Social Studies as students learn about the people and places in the world around them.

Standards Addressed:

1. World and Regional Geography

2. The Interaction of Physical and Human Systems

3. The Uses of Geography

4. Cultural Interaction

Geography is the study of the physical features of the Earth. This includes both the natural landscape and the ways that humans interact with it.

Using Maps

An important skill in the study of geography is knowing how to read and create maps. A **map** is a visual representation of a physical space. There are many types of maps, including physical maps, political maps, topographic maps, thematic maps, climate maps, historical maps, and population maps. Some key features of maps that students should know are:

- **Lines of latitude and longitude**- lines marking the distance of a location from the equator (latitude) and the prime meridian (longitude)

- **Compass rose**- symbol on a map showing the cardinal directions

- **Legend/Key**- box on a map that shows what the symbols and/or colors on a map represent

- **Scale**- Shows how distances on the map compare to real-life distances

The World in Spatial Terms

Spatial categories are used to divide the world into parts with common characteristics in order to better understand it.

The Earth is divided in halves called **hemispheres**. The Northern and Southern Hemispheres are divided by a line of latitude called the **equator**. The Eastern and Western Hemispheres are divided by a line of longitude called the **prime meridian**.

The largest masses on Earth are its seven **continents**—North America, South America, Europe, Asia, Africa, Australia, and Antarctica.

The largest bodies of water are called **oceans**. The world's oceans are the Atlantic, the Pacific, the Indian, the Arctic, and the Southern Oceans.

The world can also be divided into smaller units such as regions and places.

Regions

One way of dividing the world is into **regions**. Regions are areas that have common characteristics, both in the physical makeup of the land and in the culture of the people who live there. On the worldwide stage, some commonly identified regions include Latin America, the Middle East, and Southeast Asia.

Within the United States, the major regions are the West, the Southwest, the Midwest, the South, the Mid-Atlantic, and New England.

Places

Places are areas whose boundaries are man-made. These include countries, states, territories, counties, cities, towns, etc.

Climates and Biomes

Climates are long-term weather patterns for a particular area. The primary climates on Earth are:

- **Tropical**- hot and wet year-round
- **Dry**- temperature varies widely from day to night; very little precipitation
- **Temperate**- warm and wet in the summer, cool and dry in the winter
- **Continental**- found on large land masses, this climate has fairly low precipitation and temperatures can vary widely
- **Polar**- very cold; permanently frozen ground

Biomes are large areas that have distinct sets of plant and animal life that are well-adapted to the environment. Biomes are classified according to geography and climate. The major biomes are:

- **Alpine**- mountain regions that are cold and snowy
- **Chaparra**l- hot and dry; landscape varies- could contain plains, hills, and/or mountains
- **Deciduous forest-** contains many trees; four distinct seasons (spring, summer, fall, winter)
- **Desert-** flat land with very little precipitation

- **Grasslands**- interior flatlands with lots of grass and other low plant life; tropical or temperate climate

- **Rainforest**- tropical climate; dense vegetation

- **Savanna**- grasslands with warm temperatures year-round with a dry and a rainy season

- **Taiga**- cold, snowy winters and warm, humid summers

- **Tundra**- very cold; little vegetation; polar climate

Geographic Terms

Students will need to know important geographic terms used to describe the Earth's characteristics.

Term	Definition	Example
Archipelago	Chain of islands	Japan
Bay	A body of water that is an inlet to a larger body of water such as an ocean or a sea	San Francisco Bay
Canal	A man-made waterway	Erie Canal
Channel	A narrow body of water that connects two other bodies of water	English Channel
Delta	Low, wet, triangular piece of land at the mouth of a river	Nile Delta
Desert	Area with little to no precipitation	Sahara Desert
Gulf	A large body of water partially enclosed by land that connects to an ocean or sea	Gulf of Mexico
Island	A piece of land surrounded on all sides by water	Cuba
Isthmus	A very narrow strip of land connecting two larger pieces of land with water on both sides	Isthmus of Panama
Lake	A body of water completely surrounded by land	Lake Ontario
Mountain	A very high rocky formation	Rocky Mountains
Peninsula	A piece of land with water on three sides	Florida
Plains	Flat, grassy lands	The Great Plains
River	A long, flowing body of water that empties into a larger body of water	The Mississippi River
Sea	A large saltwater body, smaller than an ocean	Mediterranean Sea
Valley	Low area between mountains	Death Valley

Human Effects on the Environment

Humans, more than any other creatures, have the capacity to alter their environments. Human settlements have an enormous impact on the physical systems of the Earth. One major way that humans affect the natural environment is through construction. Building transportation systems, buildings, and other structures alters the landscape and displaces the organisms that once inhabited that space.

Another way humans affect the environment is by using natural resources. Earth has a limited amount of natural resources and growing human populations and advanced technology have increased the demand for those resources over time, putting a strain on the natural environment. Along with construction and the use of natural resources also comes pollution. Human activity creates waste byproducts that can be harmful to the environment.

Environmental Effects on Humans

Likewise, physical systems affects humans and they must learn to adapt to environmental factors. Physical features influence where humans will settle, what kind of communities and industries they can build there, and how easily those communities will be able to connect with other communities. For example, because of the difficult terrain, fewer people live in mountainous regions than in lowlands. Those societies that do live in the mountains have made adaptations such as terrace farming in order to survive in that environment. These communities have historically also found themselves isolated from the outside world due to the natural barriers that the mountains create.

The study of geography has many uses. It helps to make sense of the world and to picture the physical relationships between people, groups and environments. Historically, it helps people understand why societies have settled where they have and why they developed in the ways that they did. It helps to understand the causes of conflicts between bot historical and contemporary groups. It can also help to plan for the future by allowing for the examination of the distribution of people and resources throughout the world.

The study of people is found in the related fields of anthropology and sociology. **Anthropology** is the study of humans, past and present. **Sociology** looks at human social behavior, including its causes, development, and organizations. Both of these fields of study help us to understand human societies.

Throughout learning about social studies, students will encounter information about people groups, both past and present, with varied cultural backgrounds. Students should try to gain understanding of how peoples' cultural backgrounds are tied to their interactions with the world around them. This includes such topics as:

- **Environment**- How have different cultures adapted to their physical environments? How have humans altered their physical environments? Some cultures try to live in harmony with nature while others are more disruptive to the natural landscape.

- **Self**- Cultural background affects how individuals view themselves and their places in society. It affects social status, self-concept, expectations, religious beliefs, career paths, and more.

- **Family**- Family structures and relationships vary across cultures. Some societies are patriarchal (led by the eldest male) while others are matriarchal (led by the eldest female). Some cultures value filial piety (respect for elders) more than others. Culture also dictates traditions for marriage and raising children.

- **Neighborhoods and Communities**- Culture impacts the way that communities cooperate or compete. Some cultures place a high value on self-sufficiency, while others see more merit in interdependence.

At the elementary level, studies of world history are focused on those events and cultures that have most shaped our modern world. They study the lasting contributions of classical civilizations as well as recent events that have most directly contributed to the current state of modern society. Students also learn to compare and contrast as they study world cultures.

Economics is a social science concerned with how goods and services are produced, bought, and sold. Students should understand fundamental economic principles, basic components of economic systems, and the relationship between economics and society.

Standards Addressed:

1. The Major Contributions of Classical Civilizations

2. 20th Century Developments and Transformations

3. The Role of Cross-Cultural Comparisons

4. Key Terms and Basic Concepts of Economics

5. Economic Effects on Population, Resources and Technology

6. The Relationship Between Government and Economics

The Major Contributions of Classical Civilizations

Early civilizations made important achievements that have had a lasting impact on future societies. On the following pages you will find tables listing the major accomplishments of early river valley and classical civilizations, many of which are still in common use and practice today, albeit in modern form.

River Valley Civilizations

The earliest civilizations grew up in river valleys, due to the presence of fertile soil and water available for drinking, fishing, transportation, and trade. These early civilizations laid the foundations for later societies.

Civilization	Location	Major Contributions
Mesopotamian societies (e.g. Sumer, Babylon)	Tigris and Euphrates River Valley; modern-day Iraq	<ul><li>Earliest form of writing (cuneiform)</li><li>First written law code (Code of Hammurabi)</li><li>Organization into city-states</li><li>Astronomy</li></ul>
Egypt	Nile River Valley	<ul><li>Writing system (hieroglyphics)</li><li>Paper (papyrus)</li><li>Architecture (pyramids)</li><li>Strong government, military, and monetary system</li><li>Advancements in math</li></ul>
Huang He (Yellow River) Valley Civilizations	China	<ul><li>Civil service</li><li>Advancements in math and science</li></ul>
Indus Valley Civilizations	India	<ul><li>Built major cities</li><li>Advancements in math and science</li></ul>

Classical Civilizations

After the river valley civilizations paved the way for the creation of stable societies, classical civilizations emerged that were larger and stronger than their predecessors, and they would have an enormous lasting impact on future societies. These civilizations created strong governments, expanded trade, created militaries, expanded their territories, and created unified elements of culture, including religion.

Civilization	Major Characteristics and Contributions
China	<ul><li>Dynastic cycle – leaders had mandate of heaven</li><li>Elaborate bureaucracy</li><li>Religions/philosophies- Daoism and Confucianism</li><li>Advancements in math, science, and technology</li></ul>
Greece	<ul><li>Organized into city-states</li><li>Most city-states were oligarchies but Athens was a direct democracy</li><li>Polytheistic religion</li><li>High cultural period in art, poetry, philosophy, theatre, and architecture</li></ul>
Rome	<ul><li>Two major governmental periods- Republic and Empire</li><li>Unified law code- Twelve Tables</li><li>Extensive trade network</li><li>Advanced military</li><li>Engineering- aqueducts, road system</li><li>Polytheistic religion originally; later adopted Christianity</li></ul>
India	<ul><li>Caste system (rigid social class structure)</li><li>Math- concept of zero, decimal system, Arabic numerals</li><li>Religions- Hinduism and Buddhism</li><li>Advancements in medicine, including the invention of plastic surgery</li></ul>

The 1900s were a century of significant change throughout the world. It was a century full of warfare, of great technological advances, and of increasing global interconnectedness.

World War I

World War I (1914-1918) was the first truly global war. It involved nations on every continent (except Antarctica) and changed the nature of modern warfare. The long-term causes of World War I can be summarized in the acronym MAIN—militarism, alliances, imperialism, and nationalism.

- **Militarism**- Nations were building up their military personnel and weapons, both as a precautionary measure and as a sign of national prestige.

- **Alliances**- Nations began to form competing alliances. Two major alliances formed in Europe—the Tripe Alliance (Germany, Austria-Hungary, and Italy) and the Triple Entente (Great Britain, France, and Russia).

- **Imperialism**- Nations were competing for economic and political control of overseas territories.

   Nationalism- National pride was high as nations competed. Nationalist movements within nations also contributed to unrest. For example, several ethnic groups wanted independence from Austria-Hungary.

The immediate cause of World War I was the assassination of Austro-Hungarian Archduke Franz Ferdinand by a Serbian nationalist in 1914. As Austria-Hungary debated retaliation, several nations joined each side of the struggle, viewing it as an opportunity to advance their own interests, and war quickly broke out. The two sides in the war were the Allied Powers and the Central Powers.

Major Combatants in World War I

Allied Powers	Central Powers
Great Britain	Austria-Hungary
France	Germany
Russia (until 1917)	Ottoman Empire
Italy (after 1915)	Bulgaria
United States (after 1917)	

World War I included new technology and combat methods that included machine guns, airplanes, tanks, trench warfare, and submarines.

The Allied Powers won the war, which officially ended with the **Treaty of Versailles**. The treaty heavily punished Germany for its role in the war, forcing it to demilitarize and pay reparations. The **League of Nations** was established as an international peacekeeping organization but was largely ineffective, due to its inability to enforce its policies and the failure of the United States to join.

The Interwar Period

Between World War I and World War II, major events included:

- **Russian Revolution** (1917-1921)- overthrow of the Russian czar and establishment of a communist state called the Soviet Union

- **Nationalist movements** in Turkey, Iran, and Saudi Arabia

- **Spanish Civil War** (1936-1939)

- **Great Depression**- worldwide economic collapse of the 1930s

- Rise of **totalitarian** regimes in Germany (Adolf Hitler), Italy (Benito Mussolini), Spain (Francisco Franco), and the Soviet Union (Joseph Stalin)

World War II

In the 1930s, totalitarian regimes such as Germany, Italy, and the Soviet Union began to try to expand their influence outward and take over other territories. Germany invaded Czechoslovakia, Italy invaded Ethiopia, and the Soviet Union spread into Eastern Europe. Japan, too, sought territorial expansion and invaded China.

During this period, Germany, under the leadership of Hitler and the Nazi regime, perpetrated the **Holocaust**, which resulted in the death of over six million Jews and others the Nazis thought of as undesirable, including the Roma (also known as gypsies,) homosexuals, the disabled, and the mentally ill. At first, other European nations such as Britain and France practiced **appeasement**, not wanting to enter another war. This failed, however, and when Hitler invaded Poland in 1939, war broke out and many other nations joined.

Major Combatants in World War II

Allied Powers	Axis Powers
Great Britain	Germany
France	Italy
Soviet Union	Japan
United States (after 1941)	

World War II lasted from 1939 until 1945, when the United States dropped atomic bombs on Japan. The agreement that ended the war was the Treaty of Paris. The United Nations was established as an international peacekeeping organization to replace the earlier, ineffective League of Nations.

The Postwar World

Following World War II, some of the major events of the twentieth century included:

- The Cold War- a decades-long rivalry between the United States and the Soviet Union

- Communist Revolution in China (1949)

- Independence movements around the world, including India and many in Africa and the Middle East

- Ongoing Arab-Israeli conflict

- Nuclear proliferation – the worldwide spread of nuclear weapons

- Technological revolutions, including television, automobiles, computers, and the internet

Students can gain a better understanding of history through cross-cultural comparison. By comparing past cultures from around the world with one another, students can gain an understanding of commonalities, differences, and global patterns.

By comparing past cultures with modern ones, students can see the progression that societies have made over time, understand how civilizations have built on the achievements of those that have come before, and gain a more thorough understanding of both past and present societies.

Students should be familiar with the basic concepts and key terms related to the study of economics.

There are two major division of economics—macroeconomics and microeconomics. **Macroeconomics** is the study of how economics works on a large scale, such as in a whole nation. **Microeconomics** is the study of economics on a smaller scale, looking at the decisions and impacts of individuals, small groups, and specific markets.

Resources are limited (**scarcity**), so people must make choices about how those resources will be allocated. On a small scale, individuals make choices about what they will buy and sell. On a larger scale, societies create economic systems that determine how goods will be produced, bought, and sold and by whom.

Economic Systems

Capitalism is a system in which property and the means of production are privately owned. What is produced, how much, and at what price is dictated by the market forces of **supply and demand**. If demand for a product is high, the supply will run low and prices will increase. If demand is low, the supply will be high and prices will decrease. The **profit motive** encourages hard work and innovation. Capitalism is also called a **market economy**. The purest form of capitalism is **laissez-faire**, in which the government takes a completely hands-off approach to the economic sector and allows market forces to regulate themselves.

Socialism is a system in which property is controlled collectively rather than individually. The purest form of socialism is **communism**, in which everything is owned in common and there is no private property and no social classes. In theory, communism eventually replaces the need for a government. In reality, however, nations that practice forms of communism tend to have very strong governments that take complete economic control. An economy in which the government has total control of the economy through centralized planning is called a **command** or a **planned economy**.

A **mixed economy** is a blend of capitalist and socialist principles, with both publicly and privately owned business operating at the same time. A **closed economy** is one that is self-sufficient and cut off from outside influences, while an **open economy** allows for trade with other nations.

A **subsistence economy** is one in which people only produce that which is needed to survive.

Key Terms

Other important terms in the study of economics include:

- **Balance of trade-** a measure of a nation's exports vs. imports

- **Budget-** planning how current money will be allocated

- **Consumption-** the use of resources

- **Deflation-** an overall decrease in the price of goods and services

- **Depression-** a long period of economic decline, usually marked by inflation, high unemployment, and industrial decline

- **Exports-** goods sold to another country

- **Imports-** goods bought from another country

- **Inflation-** an overall increase in the price of goods and services

- **Profit-** the difference between revenue and cost

- **Recession-** a period of slow economic growth

- **Shortage-** when demand exceeds supply

- **Surplus-** when supply exceeds demand

Economic Effects on Population, Resources and Technology

There are close relationships between economics, population, resources, and technology. Human populations are greatly affected by the availability of resources. An area must have sufficient resources to sustain its population or the society cannot survive. Where resources are scarce, people must either obtain resources from outside sources or migrate to areas with sufficient resources. In some cases, societies also work to control the population and limit its growth.

As populations grow and technology becomes more advanced, humanity has used more and more resources. As these resources are increasingly scarce, control of resources is important and the trade of resources a vital part of the global economy.

Technology has made the global economy evermore connected. Advances in transportation and communication technologies have allowed for business to be conducted in worldwide markets in ways never previously possible.

The Relationship Between Government and Economics

Different nations use different economic systems and therefore have different levels of governmental involvement in the economic sectors. A command economy gives the government complete control over economic decision-making, while a laissez-faire system allows the government no role and leaves economic decisions up to individuals and market forces. Most nations' systems are somewhere in the middle of these two extremes.

The United States is primarily a market economy but it does allow the government a degree of regulatory control. The government attempts to intervene in ways that will create a healthy, growing economic environment. Government involvement includes taxation, setting interest rates, regulating the monetary supply, regulating trade, and providing oversight.

Science

Scientific knowledge is an essential part of students' academic foundation for life. Students develop skills in critical thinking, problem solving, and scientific methodology while learning about natural, physical, and chemical processes.

Test Structure

The Science subtest consists of 50 multiple choice questions and lasts for 50 minutes. Within Science, there are three major subcategories with which you must be familiar:

A. Earth Science (32% of Science content)

B. Life Science (34% of Science content)

C. Physical Science (34% of Science content)

Each subcategory is divided into standards that state the skills you must be able to demonstrate on the exam.

Earth Science

Earth science is the study of the Earth, its composition, its history, its place in the universe, and its natural processes.

Standards Addressed:

1. The Structure of the Earth System
2. The Processes of the Earth System
3. The Earth's History
4. The Earth and the Universe
5. The Earth's Patterns, Cycles, and Change
6. Science as a Human Endeavor, a Process, and a Career
7. Science as Inquiry
8. How to Use Resources and Research Material in Science
9. The Unifying Processes of Science

Both Earth itself and the air surrounding it exist in layers. These layers have different properties that work together to create an environment that can sustain life.

Layers of the Earth

- **Inner core**- the spherical solid center of the Earth, composed largely of iron and nickel; about 700-800 miles in diameter

- **Outer core**- a layer of liquid iron and nickel about 1,400 miles thick

- **Mantle**- a layer of hot, semi-solid rock about 1,800 miles thick that has currents, causing the plates of crust on top of it to move

- **Crust**- a series of solid plates that cover the Earth's surface, ranging from 5 to 30 miles thick

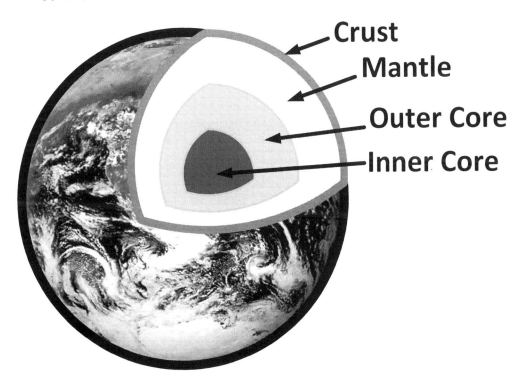

The crust consists of **continental** (land) plates and **oceanic** plates. These plates are constantly shifted atop the mantle. The movement of these plates is known as **plate tectonics**.

The boundaries between plates help to shape the Earth's surface and can cause geological events. There are three ways plates can interact at their boundaries:

Type of Boundary	Example	Results
Convergent (colliding)	→ ←	Mountains, ridges, volcanoes
Divergent (separating)	← →	Bodies of water, new crust
Transform (rubbing)	↑ ↓	Earthquakes

Layers of the Atmosphere

The **atmosphere** (the air above Earth) also exists in layers.

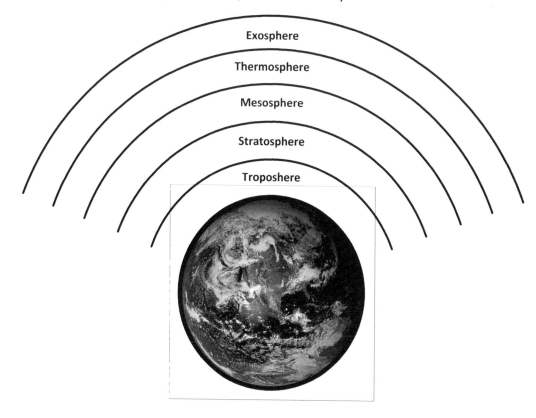

Exosphere

Thermosphere

Mesosphere

Stratosphere

Troposhere

The Earth operates according to several systems and processes, all of which are interrelated and work together to create an environment in which life is sustainable.

Heat

Heat is a process that greatly affects everything else on Earth. The Earth's heat comes from:

- **Radioactivity** at the Earth's core, which is responsible for the movement of plates and thus the creation of landforms.

- **Solar energy**, which heats Earth's surface.

  - The **tilt** of the Earth on its **axis** determines the amount of direct radiation from the sun at any given point on Earth. Locations closest to the equator receive the most direct solar rays and are therefore warmer throughout the year than the poles.

  - The **rotation** of the Earth is responsible for night and day and the gain and loss of heat and sunlight that accompany those times of day.

  - The **revolution** of the Earth around the sun is responsible for the changing of the seasons.

Geological Processes

Geological processes are processes at work on the Earth's landforms. There are three major types of rocks:

Type of Rock	Description	Examples
Igneous	Formed through the cooling of magma	Granite, obsidian, pumice
Sedimentary	Formed when sediments (bits of eroded rock, sand, shells, fossils, etc.) are compressed into hard layers over time	Sandstone, limestone, shale
Metamorphic	Formerly igneous and sedimentary rocks that have morphed due to heat and pressure	Marble, quartzite, slate

These rock layers that make up the Earth's surface can change over time through forces such as weathering and erosion. **Weathering** is the breaking down of rock via natural forces such as water, ice, wind, and the sun. **Erosion** is when pieces of the weathered material are carried away via wind and water.

The **rock cycle** describes how rocks are created, changed, and destroyed.

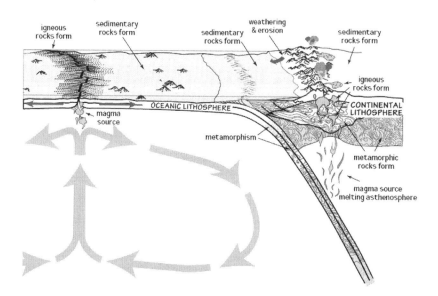

Water Cycle

The **water cycle** shows how water circulates through the Earth's surface and atmosphere.

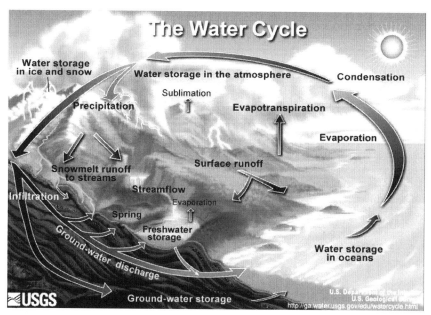

Geological history is the study of how Earth has developed over time. The Earth is estimated to be between 4 and 5 billion years old. Over the course of its history, the Earth's landforms and life forms have undergone a great deal of change.

The Geologic Record

The **geologic record** helps scientists to learn about different parts of the Earth's history by examining layers of rock. Scientists base their findings on the **law of superposition**, which says that the oldest rocks are found at the bottom and newer rocks are found at the top. This helps scientists to date events and create a timeline of Earth's history.

The Earth's history is divided into two major time periods called eons:

Precambrian Eon	Phanerozoic Eon		
From the beginning of the Earth to the formation of life	• From the formation of life to the present day • Divided into three eras:		
	Paleozoic Era	**Mesozoic Era**	**Cenozoic Era**
	• Approx. 542-251 million years ago • Rise of early life including trilobites, shellfish, corals, sponges, fish, land plants like ferns and trees, insects, amphibians, and reptiles	• Approx. 251-65 million years ago • Rise of dinosaurs, mammals, birds, and flowering plants • Also later included the extinction of dinosaurs	• Approx. 65 million years ago to present day • Rise of primates, including hominids and eventually modern humans

Paleontology is the study of fossils. These scientists can study the origins and history of life by looking at the fossils contained within the layers of rock that compose the Earth. The evolution of life will be examined in greater detail in the Life Science section.

The Universe and its Origins

The Earth is just one among many bodies in the **universe**. The universe is thought to be approximately 20 billion years old. The **Big Bang Theory** states that the universe was created when a large collection of matter exploded, sending pieces of it that would become the planets, stars and other bodies expanding outward.

Galaxies

Galaxies are systems of stars. The Earth belongs to the **Milky Way Galaxy**.

Astronomers (scientists who study celestial bodies) keep track of stars by organizing them into **constellations**.

Solar Systems

Within galaxies are solar systems, which consist of planets and other bodies orbiting a star. Our **solar system** consists of eight planets that orbit around the sun in elliptical patterns.

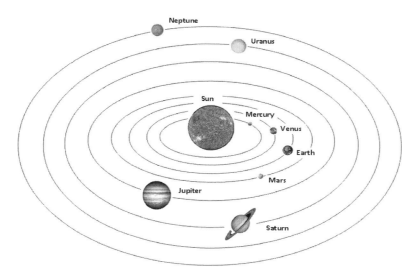

Moons

Moons revolve around planets, held in orbit by gravity. Some planets have more than one moon, but the Earth only has one, known as the Moon.

It takes the Moon 28 days to revolve around the Earth. The Moon does not give off any light of its own, but reflects light from the sun. Depending on the position of the Moon and the Earth in relationship to the sun, the Moon looks different from Earth at different times of the month. These are called the **phases of the Moon**.

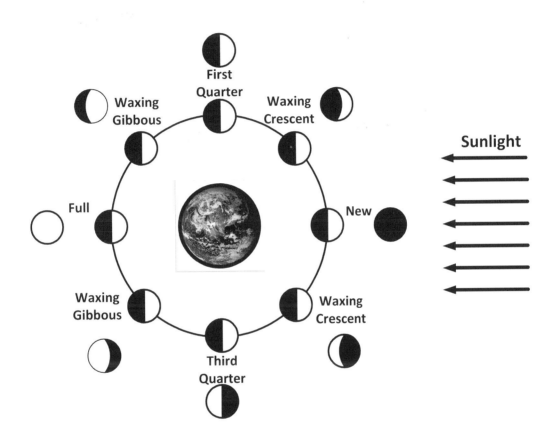

Eclipses are special events in which the sun, Moon, and Earth all line up in a direct path.

In a **solar eclipse**, the Moon is directly between the sun and the Earth and casts a shadow on the Earth's surface.

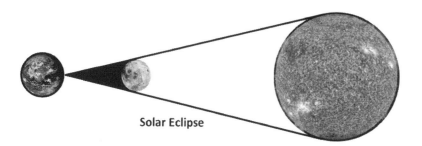

Solar Eclipse

In a **lunar eclipse**, the Earth is directly between the sun and the Moon, blocking light from hitting the Moon.

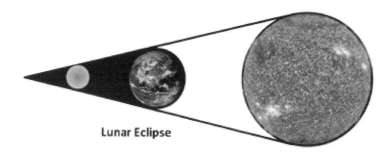

Lunar Eclipse

Other Celestial Objects

There are other objects in space besides stars, planets, and moons. Some of these include:

- **Asteroids**- large rocky objects in space; there is a large asteroid belt between Mars and Jupiter

- **Meteoroids**- smaller rocky or metallic objects travelling through space

- **Meteorites**- meteoroids that enter Earth's atmosphere

  - **Meteors** are streaks of light that trail behind meteorites as they burn in Earth's atmosphere

- **Comets**- icy bodies that form tails as they near the sun

Earth is constantly changing. Some changes occur over long periods of time, while others take place in a relatively short period of time. Likewise, some changes are permanent whereas others are cyclical.

Long-Term Changes

These are some of the ways in which the Earth has gradually changed over its long history:

- **Plate tectonics** have caused the movement of Earth's continental and oceanic plates. Over time, this has resulted in significant changes to both the composition and the location of Earth's landforms.
    - Scientists speculate that the continents were once all connected in a large landmass called Pangaea, and that they have separated over time to create our modern continents.
    - Shifting of plates causes the creation and destruction of mountains, valleys, and bodies of water.
- **Evolution** of life forms from the simplest life to the rise of modern humans

Short-Term Changes, Patterns, and Cycles

- **Water cycle**- the circulation of water through the Earth's surface and atmosphere (see the Processes of the Earth System section)
- **Weather**- the state of the atmosphere at a particular time and place, including temperature, air movement, precipitation, and humidity
- **Seasons**- four phases of the year caused by the Earth's revolution around the sun, marked by differences in weather patterns

Science as a Human Endeavor, a Process and a Career

Science is a process shared by all humanity as they try to gain knowledge of the world. Careers in science are plentiful and include a wide variety of areas, including medicine, engineering, environmental science, astronomy, geology, computer science, science education, meteorology, biochemistry, and so many more. Students should be introduced to practical applications and careers in science in order to maintain a real world connection with the content they are learning.

Science is the process by which we gain new knowledge of how the world works. The process is one of inquiry, wherein people ask questions about the world and make observations and perform experiments in order to find the answers to those questions.

The Scientific Method

The main process used in scientific inquiry is known as the Scientific Method. This lays out the proper steps for scientific investigations.

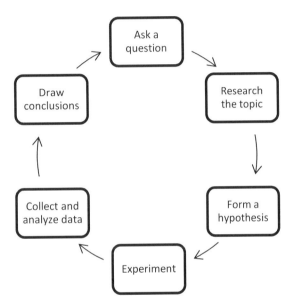

How to Use Resources and Research Material in Science

There are many resources available to teachers in science. Teacher should use, and encourage their students to use, scholarly research on scientific topics. Resource materials can be found in books, in journals, and online. Students should be taught to evaluate the reliability of source materials. This is especially important with online resources. Research should be well-documented and come from a reputable source. Students should be encouraged to read with a critical eye.

An important part of science is finding a way to organize information. There are some universal methods that scientists use to organize data from their experiments and observations. This helps to unify science because it makes it easier for scientists to communicate and share their ideas.

Systems

A **system** is a group of related parts that are organized to create a unified whole, serving a common purpose. Some examples of systems include ecosystems, body systems, solar systems, and mechanical systems. There are two main types of systems—closed and open.

- A **closed system** does not interact with other systems. It does not allow certain types of transfers in or out of the system.

- An **open system** is one that continuously interacts with its surroundings.

Order

Order is a way of describing behavior using statistics. An example of order is probability.

Organization

Organization refers to ways of putting data into structures. Some examples of organization include the Periodic Table and the taxonomy for organism classification.

Life science is the study of living things on Earth, including their characteristics, biological processes, behaviors, history, and relationships.

Standards Addressed:

1. The Structure and Function of Living Systems
2. Reproduction and Heredity
3. Change Over Time in Living Things
4. Regulation and Behavior
5. Adaptation, Classification, Unity and Diversity of Life
6. The Interdependence of Organisms
7. Personal Health

Characteristics of Living Things

Living things share several common traits:

- Use energy

- Are capable of growth

- Reproduce

- Have definite life spans

- Respond and adapt to their environment

- They are made up of **cells**

- Cells are organized in the following manner:

    o **Tissue**- a group of cells

    o **Organ**- a group of tissues working together for a common purpose

    o **Organ system**- a group of organs working together

    o **Organism**- a complete living thing, made up of systems

Cells

Living things are made up of cells. The purposes of cells are to create energy for the organism, to create proteins, and to reproduce. Plant cells and animal cells share many similarities but plant cells contain some parts that animal cells do not.

Parts of Plant and Animal Cells	
Part	**Function**
Nucleus	Control center of the cell which contains DNA
Cytoplasm	Everything outside the nucleus
Endoplasmic reticulum	Transport system for molecules between the nucleus and the cytoplasm
Ribosomes	Make proteins
Golgi bodies	Package and transport proteins
Mitochondria	Create energy (ATP)
Vacuoles	Store food and water
Lysosomes	The digestive system of the cell; holds enzymes that are used to break down molecules
Cell membrane	Permeable boundary of the cell that allows the passage of needed materials in and waste out

Parts Only Found in Plant Cells	
Chloroplasts	Contain chlorophyll, used in food production
Cell wall	Rigid outer structure of the cell

Animal cell:

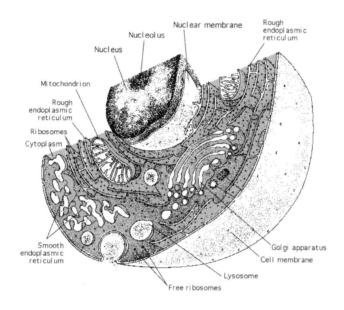

Plant cell:

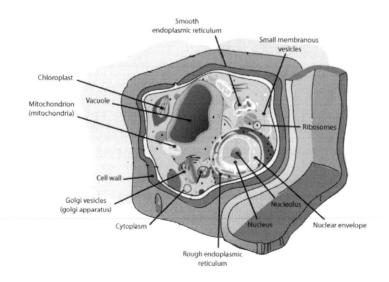

Structure of Plants

Part	Function
Roots	Hold the plant into the ground; absorb water and nutrients from the soil
Stem	Carry nutrients from the roots to the rest of the plant
Leaves	Make food for the plant through **photosynthesis**, a process by which the plant uses its chlorophyll, water, nutrients, carbon dioxide, and energy from the sun to make food and oxygen
Flower	Site of reproduction

Structure of Animals

Animals' organ systems provide the basic functions which enable them to live. While animals all possess some form of these systems, the organs they contain may differ among species. The chart below contains information about each system and provides the names of some of the human body parts for these systems.

System	Function	Contents in Humans
Digestive	Provides nutrition to the body	Mouth, tongue, esophagus, stomach, large and small intestines
Circulatory	Carries blood throughout the body	Heart, veins, arteries
Respiratory	Brings in oxygen and expels carbon dioxide	Nose, mouth, trachea, lungs
Excretory	Eliminates waste	Skin, kidneys, bladder
Nervous	Carries electrical signals from brain to the cells	Brain, nerves
Reproductive	Creates offspring	Male and female reproductive organs
Muscular and/or Skeletal	Provides structure and allows movement	Muscles, bones
Regulatory	Regulates body functions	Pancreas, thyroid, brain

Reproduction is the creation of new organisms of the same species. Reproduction is essential for the continuation of the species. **DNA** (deoxyribonucleic acid) contains the codes for proteins, which are the building blocks of life. DNA is made up of two strands that contain **genes** that dictate traits for an organism. Groups of genes make up **chromosomes**.

Organisms reproduce using one of two types of reproduction:

1. **Asexual reproduction**- New cells are created from only one parent organism via cells that produce two identical sets of chromosomes and then split to form new cells.

2. **Sexual reproduction**- Reproduction involves two parent organisms, each of whom contribute a reproductive cell containing one set of chromosomes. The two combine to create cells with a full set of chromosomes.

Chromosomes come in pairs and each half of the pair comes with genes for each trait. The combination of these genes determine the organism's traits. Traits can be classified as either **dominant** or **recessive**.

Dominant genes are more likely to appear in an organism. Recessive genes will generally be hidden by dominant genes if dominant genes are also present.

If there are two dominant genes, the dominant trait will appear in the organism. If there is one dominant and one recessive gene, the dominant trait will appear in the organism. If both genes are recessive, the recessive trait will appear in the organism.

For example, brown eyes are a trait that is dominant over blue eyes. If each parent contributes genes for both brown (B) and blue (b) eyes, the possibilities for the child will be:

	B	b
B	BB	Bb
b	Bb	bb

If even one dominant trait (B) is present in a pair, it will appear in the organism, therefore, in three out of the four possible combinations of genes for this child (75%), the child will have brown eyes.

Living things change over time. This includes changes within the lifetime of a single organism, as well as long-term changes in the history of a species.

Life Cycles

One of the characteristics of a living thing is that it has a finite life span. Every organism goes through a life cycle, made up of the various stages that are common to all living things:

1. The organism comes into existence

2. Growth

3. Metamorphosis

4. Maturation

5. Reproduction

6. Death

Biological Evolution

The way that species change over time is through biological evolution. Most of the times, offspring have genes like their parents. Occasionally, however, mistakes in the DNA duplication process result in abnormalities called mutations. Most mutations are benign and some are negative, but sometimes a mutation actually has a positive effect for the organism. A positive mutation may make it easier for the organism to survive and reproduce. When this happens, the process of natural selection makes it so that eventually, most of the members of that species will come to possess the favorable mutation.

Natural selection is the process by which those traits that are beneficial to organisms are produced and passed on in the species. Natural selection is based on a premise of the "survival of the fittest," which says that those organisms best genetically equipped to survive and reproduce will survive and will have their traits passed on. Those organisms that are weaker will eventually die off and with them, their less favorable traits.

Over time, the process of natural selection can result in significant changes to a species.

The Earth consists of many diverse environments, and organisms on Earth must regulate themselves and adapt to those environments when necessary. Some of the adaptations and means of self-regulation that organisms implement are:

- Life cycles (see standard 3)

- Natural selection and evolution (see standard 3)

- The organization of the food chain (see standard 6)

- Cooperation and competition within ecosystems (see standard 6)

- Reactions to limited resources

- In the case of humans, altering the environment

There are millions of species of organisms on Earth. Scientists have come up with a way of classifying these organisms, a system called a **taxonomy**. All organisms are first classified as belonging to one of five **kingdoms**:

1. **Monera**- single-celled organisms with no cell nuclei, such as bacteria

2. **Protista**- single-celled organisms that do have cell nuclei, such as algae and protozoa

3. **Fungi**- can be single or multi-cellular; includes mushrooms, mold, lichen, and yeast

4. **Plantae**- multi-cellular plants

5. **Animalia**- multi-cellular animals

From there, each kingdom is further broken down into subcategories. The levels of the taxonomy are:

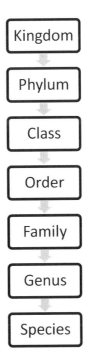

Each level groups organisms by common characteristics, with traits getting more specific the further down the classification system you go.

As an example, humans are classified as follows:

- Kingdom: animalia (animals)

- Phylum: chordata (vertebrates)

- Class: mammalia (mammals)

- Order: primates (monkeys, apes, etc.)

- Family: hominids (great apes)

- Genus: *Homo* (humans and their closest genetic ancestors)

- Species: *Homo sapiens* (modern humans)

Species can adapt to their environment, which can result in genetic change over time, resulting in the evolution of different species (see the Changes Over Time in Living Things section).

Organisms all share space on the Earth and must therefore live in cooperation in order to survive. The **biosphere** is the environment on Earth in which living things exist. It includes the land, the water, and the air.

Within the biosphere are smaller environments, known as ecosystems. An **ecosystem** is a community of organisms and their physical environment. An ecosystem requires an energy source (such as the sun), a means to convert that energy to glucose (plant life), and a means of recycling organic materials.

Ecosystems operate and transfer energy according to a cycle:

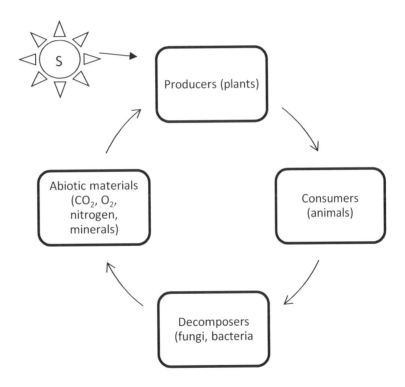

The Food Chain

The way that energy moves through living things in an ecosystem is through the **food chain**. The food chain describes the order in which animals consume plants and other animals.

Plants create energy in the form of ATP through photosynthesis. They are known as **producers**. To get this energy for themselves, animals must either eat those plants (herbivores) or eat another animal (carnivore), which somewhere down the line has eaten a plant and gotten its energy.

Animals are known as **consumers** because they consume (eat) other organisms. Those who eat plants are known as primary consumers. Those who eat primary consumers are known as secondary consumers, etc. At the highest level of a food chain are those top consumers who have few natural predators and are therefore unlikely to be eaten.

Here is an example of a food chain in an ecosystem:

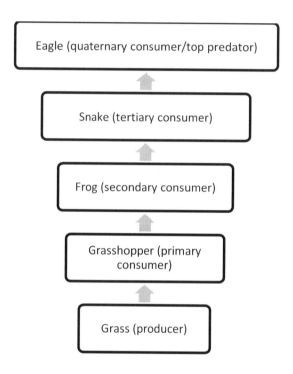

Disruptions to Ecosystems

The balance of ecosystems is delicate and can be disrupted by many causes that include:

- Interruptions in the food chain

- Depletion of any species

- Natural disasters

- Change in energy supply

- Human causes, such as pollution, deforestation, depletion of resources, mining, and radiation

The components of personal health that elementary students need to be aware of include nutrition, communicable diseases, and substance abuse.

Nutrition

Nutrition tells students how to eat in a way that is healthy. Food is required to provide energy that the body needs to carry on its functions. Eating healthy foods provides the body with the best possible energy. Three basic components of food are protein, carbohydrates, and fat.

- **Proteins** assist with muscle growth.

- **Carbohydrates** provide energy.

- **Fat** is stored for the body to use when it doesn't get enough food.

Foods come in five basic groups—grains, meats, dairy, fruits, and vegetables. (Sweets and other innutritious foods are considered empty calories and are not a part of these food groups.) A healthy diet includes a balance of these groups. Students should also be aware of some of the adverse effects of not maintaining a nutritious diet, including obesity, heart disease, and diabetes.

Communicable Diseases

Communicable diseases are those illnesses that can be spread from person to person. Students should learn the important steps in communicable disease prevention.

Personal hygiene, such as hand washing, covering the mouth when coughing or sneezing, and general cleanliness can help prevent the spread of communicable diseases.

Some diseases are also prevented through the use of **vaccinations**, which help people develop a resistance to a disease by putting a small amount of an inactive virus into the person's body, allowing the immune system to create antibodies against it.

Substance Abuse

Drugs and alcohol are substances that can be harmful to the body. Even legal drugs like medicine can be harmful if used improperly. There are three basic categories of drugs—stimulants, depressants, and hallucinogens.

Type of Drug	Examples	Effects on the Body
Stimulants	Nicotine, caffeine, cocaine, amphetamines, ecstasy, meth	Elevated mood, high followed by a crash, paranoia, restlessness, irritability
Depressants	Alcohol, heroin, morphine, codeine, barbiturates, tranquilizers, marijuana	Depressed central nervous system, slow responses, reduced pain, reduced inhibitions
Hallucinogens	LSD, PCP, psilocybin	Altered mental perception, hallucinations

Physical science is the study of the physical and chemical materials, processes, and forces that make up our environment.

Standards Addressed:

1. The Properties and Structure of Matter

2. Forces and Motions

3. Energy

4. Interactions Between Energy and Matter

Matter is the physical substance of which everything is composed. Matter comes in many different varieties and can even change forms.

The most basic unit of matter is the **atom**. An atom is made up of a center cluster of positively charged **protons** and non-charged **neutrons** called a **nucleus**, as well as outer layers of negatively charged **electrons.**

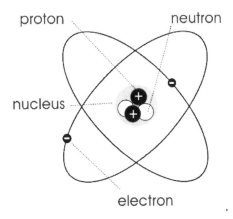

An **element** is a type of substance that cannot be broken down into different types of matter. Currently there are 114 known elements and they are listed by atomic number in the **periodic table**.

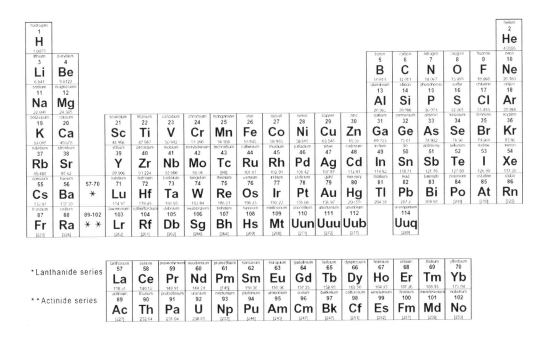

Elements combine in different ways to make up all matter. Two or more atoms combined into an electrically neutral structure are called a **molecule**. Molecules can contain atoms that are of the same element or of different elements. A **compound** is the chemical bonding of two or more different elements.

Different materials can also combine without altering their molecular composition. Two methods of combination are through mixtures and solutions. **Mixtures** occur when two unlike substances are mixed together without a chemical reaction. **Solutions** occur when one type of substance dissolves into another.

States of Matter

Matter can exist in three forms or states—solid, liquid, and gas.

- **Solids** have molecules that are relatively close together and have strong molecular forces that hold the substance into a fixed shape with a fixed volume.

- **Liquids** have weaker molecular forces than solids, which allow them to move fluidly and take on the shape of their container, while still maintaining a fixed volume.

- **Gases** have weak molecular bonds which allow the molecules to move rapidly. Gases take on both the shape and volume of their containers, as they will spread out as far as their container will allow.

Matter can change its state through changes in temperature and pressure.

From	To	Name of Change
Solid	Liquid	Melting
Solid	Gas	Sublimation
Liquid	Gas	Vaporization
Liquid	Solid	Freezing
Gas	Liquid	Condensation
Gas	Solid	Deposition

The **Law of Conservation of Matter** states that matter can be neither created nor destroyed, but it can be rearranged. Physical changes like these phase changes and chemical changes, such as the creation of compounds, are just some of the many ways that matter can be changed.

Motion

Motion is change is an object's position. The fundamental principles of motion are those found in **Newton's Laws of Motion**. His three laws are:

1. An object in motion will stay in motion and an object at rest will stay at rest until acted upon by an outside force. (**inertia**)

2. An object will move in the direction of the force that was applied to it, with an acceleration proportional to the force applied. Force = mass x acceleration

3. For every action, there is an equal and opposite reaction.

Force

Force is an influence that causes an object to undergo a change in motion. There are different types:

Type	Definition
Applied Force	Force applied directly to an object by another object or person (e.g. pushing and pulling)
Gravity	The force with which a massively large object (such as the Earth or another planet or moon) pulls other, smaller objects toward itself ; gravity on Earth pulls everything toward the Earth's center
Friction	The force exerted by an object or surface as another object slides across it
Air Resistance	Force exerted upon objects as they move through the air
Normal Force	The support force applied when an object comes is in contact with another stable object
Tension Force	Force present in a cable when pulled on both ends
Spring Force	The force a spring exerts on any object attached to it
Electromagnetic Force	A natural force that affects electrically charged particles

When the result of all forces acting on an object is zero, the object is said to be in **equilibrium** and is either at rest or is in unaccelerated motion.

Energy

Energy is defined as the ability to do work. Energy comes in several different forms, including kinetic, potential, thermal, radiant, electrical, mechanical, chemical, and nuclear. While energy cannot be created or destroyed (**Law of Conservation of Energy**) it can be transferred to another form.

Kinetic and Potential Energy

The two most basic states of energy are kinetic and potential. **Kinetic energy** is energy in motion. **Potential energy** is stored energy that can be converted to kinetic energy. An object in motion has kinetic energy, while an object at rest has potential energy.

Thermal Energy

Thermal energy (or **heat**) is the energy of a substance or system related to its temperature. Heat is caused by the vibration of molecules. The faster the vibration, the more heat will be produced.

Heat can be transferred in three major ways:

1. **Conduction**- heat transfer via a conductive material such as metal

2. **Convection**- heat transfer through the collision of liquid or gas molecules

3. **Radiation**- heat is transmitted without contact via infrared radiation

Radiant Energy

Radiant energy is the energy of electromagnetic waves such as light.

Electric Energy

Electric energy is a form of energy that is delivered or absorbed by an electrical circuit. An **electrical circuit** is the path along which an electrical current flows.

Conductors are those materials that allow electrical current to flow through them, such as metals. **Insulators** are those materials that do not allow the flow of electrical currents, such as plastic and wood.

Mechanical Energy

Mechanical energy is related to the use of machines. The most basic types of machines are known as **simple machines**. These systems perform work with very few parts.

There are six basic types of simple machines:

Simple Machine	Description	Example
Incline Plane	Used to help move things up or down by reducing the force needed by increasing the distance	
Lever	Used to lift a load using applied force and a fulcrum or pivot	
Pulley	A system that uses a wheel and a rope to make it easier to lift things	
Screw	An inclined plane wrapped around a pole that can be used for holding objects together or for lifting	
Wedge	An object with at least one slanting side resulting in a very narrow edge, used to separate or cut things	
Wheel and Axle	Allows objects to move more quickly and easily by rolling them	

Chemical Energy

Chemical energy is the energy stored in the bonds between atoms in molecules. Chemical energy contains the potential for a **chemical reaction**, wherein one set of chemical substances is transformed into another.

Nuclear Energy

Nuclear energy results from a change in the nucleus of atoms. There are two types of nuclear reactions. When nuclei are split, this is called **fission**. Fission is the type of reaction used in creating atomic bombs and nuclear reactors. The joining of nuclei is called **fusion**, which occurs in the sun and in hydrogen bombs.

Energy can interact with matter in a variety of ways.

Electricity

Electricity moves through matter (specifically, a conductor) as a current. Electricity can produce light, heat, motion, and magnetic force.

Electricity can be measured in terms of voltage and amperage. **Voltage** is a measure of the amount of force in an electrical current. **Amperage** measures the strength of an electrical current as it passes through a conductor.

Magnetism

Magnetism involves the forces exerted by magnets on other magnets. All magnets have two poles (called "North" and "South") which have opposite charges. Opposite poles attract one another, while similar poles repel.

Sound

Sound moves in waves caused by the vibrations of particles. The three major characteristics of sound are pitch, amplitude, and quality. Differences in **pitch** are cause by the rate of the vibrations. The faster the vibrations, the higher the pitch. **Amplitude** is how loud a sound is, which is caused by the force used to create the sound. The greater the force that created the sound, the louder the sound will be. Sound **quality** is also known as timbre and includes other characteristics that allow the ear to distinguish between sounds of the same pitch and amplitude.

Practice Examination

Reading and Language Arts

1. When evaluating media sources, an important consideration is

    A. format

    B. bias

    C. message

    D. all of the above

2. Which of these is NOT an example of critical comprehension

    A. determining an author's tone

    B. distinguishing fact from opinion

    C. identifying the topic sentence of a passage

    D. recognizing bias

3. The purpose of an editorial is typically

    A. to entertain

    B. to inform

    C. to persuade

    D. to teach

Questions 4-5 refer to the following passage:

JULIET: (to Romeo) Good night, good night! parting is such sweet sorrow,
That I shall say good night till it be morrow.
-From *Romeo and Juliet* by William Shakespeare

4. These lines contain

    A. end rhyme

    B. repetition

    C. iambic pentameter

    D. all of the above

5. The passage above is an example of

    A. monologue

    B. soliloquy

    C. dialogue

    D. prose

6. Which of these is considered a form of drama?

    A. allegory

    B. puppetry

    C. novel

    D. parable

7. Anne Frank's diary is a(n)

    A. novel

    B. sonnet

    C. allegory

    D. primary source

8. Novels, short stories, and plays are common forms of

    A. poetry

    B. non-fiction

    C. expository writing

    D. narratives

9. Which of these distinguishes poetry from prose?

    A. Metaphor

    B. Narrative

    C. Verse

    D. Allusion

10. "Pretty ugly" is an example of a(n)

    A. onomatopoeia

    B. oxymoron

    C. allusion

    D. hyperbole

11. Which of these language techniques tends to be the most difficult for many second language learners to understand?

    A. Imagery

    B. Idiom

    C. Alliteration

    D. Simile

12. Identify the antecedent in the following sentence: "Julia drank coffee while she worked on the report."

    A. Julia

    B. drank

    C. she

    D. report

13. Which of the following is an example of hyperbole?

    A. She was as clever as a fox.

    B. I've been waiting in this line forever.

    C. The bright blue balloon floated away.

    D. It was a real Cinderella story.

14. An editorial is an example of

    A. descriptive writing

    B. expository writing

    C. persuasive writing

    D. narrative writing

15. Which of these words does NOT contain an affix?

A. Bicycle

B. Largest

C. Start

D. Prediction

16. "The stars danced in the night sky" is an example of

A. personification

B. onomatopoeia

C. allusion

D. simile

Question 17 refers to the following passage:

"Hickory, Dickory, Dock,
The mouse ran up the clock."

17. The lines above best demonstrate

A. assonance

B. alliteration

C. consonance

D. end rhyme

18. A question mark is most likely to be used in which type of sentence?

A. Declarative

B. Interrogative

C. Imperative

D. Exclamatory

19. The type of narrator that can explain the thoughts of any character is

A. Omniscient

B. First person

C. Limited omniscient

D. Second person

20. **While speaking, Ms. King is looking for signs that her students are listening. Which of the following non-verbal cues gives the impression of effective listening?**

    A. Maintaining eye contact with Ms. King

    B. Packing up supplies in backpacks

    C. Immediately raising a hand to ask a question while Ms. King is still speaking

    D. Putting heads down on desks

21. **The turning point of a story is known as the**

    A. exposition

    B. conflict

    C. setting

    D. climax

22. **Which of the following would be the best topic sentence for a persuasive essay?**

    A. World War II was a fight between the Axis and the Allies.

    B. World War II took place between 1939 and 1945.

    C. The use of the atomic bomb during World War II was not justified.

    D. New technologies were used in World War II.

Questions 23-25 refer to the following passage:

"Tom appeared on the sidewalk with a bucket of whitewash and a long-handled brush. He surveyed the fence, and all gladness left him and a deep melancholy settled down upon his spirit. Thirty yards of board fence nine feet high. Life to him seemed hollow, and existence but a burden. Sighing, he dipped his brush and passed it along the topmost plank; repeated the operation; did it again; compared the insignificant whitewashed streak with the far-reaching continent of unwhitewashed fence, and sat down on a tree-box discouraged."
                    -From *The Adventures of Tom Sawyer* by Mark Twain

23. **In this passage, Tom appears to be**

    A. dedicated

    B. reluctant

    C. motivated

    D. inventive

24. **If a student were unfamiliar with the word "melancholy," which word(s) in the passage might provide the best context clue as to its meaning?**

    A. "upon his spirit"
    B. "far-reaching"
    C. "insignificant"
    D. "gladness left him"

25. **The comparison of the "insignificant whitewashed streak" to the "far-reaching continent of unwhitewashed fence" is used to**

    A. provide a precise measurement of the painted area
    B. demonstrate how hard Tom had been working
    C. emphasize the perceived enormity of Tom's task
    D. portray Tom as unintelligent

26. **"My daughter's doll" is an example of a(n)**

    A. dependent clause
    B. independent clause
    C. phrase
    D. declarative sentence

27. **Effective listening involves**

    A. focusing on the speaker
    B. paying attention to nonverbal cues
    C. responding appropriately
    D. all of the above

28. **Which of these does NOT contain meter?**

    A. Blank verse
    B. Limerick
    C. Free verse
    D. Sonnet

29. **Rhyming and segmenting are examples of**

    A. phonological awareness skills
    B. concept of print
    C. decoding
    D. alphabetic principles

30. **Identify the error in the following sentence: "Lily and me went on vacation together."**

    A. It is an independent clause.
    B. It is a dependent clause.
    C. It uses an object pronoun instead of a subject pronoun.
    D. It uses a subject pronoun instead of an object pronoun.

31. **Which of these skills is typically the first to develop?**

    A. Syllabication
    B. Decoding
    C. Fluency
    D. Letter-sound correspondence

32. **After reading the story of the "Three Little Pigs," a student summarizes the story by saying, "The only pig whose house wasn't blown down by the wolf was the one who built his house out of bricks." This student is demonstrating**

    A. critical comprehension
    B. literal comprehension
    C. metacognition
    D. phonological awareness

33. **Identify the error in the following sentences: "Maria moved to New York City last month. She lived in Brooklyn where she works in a café."**

    A. Subject-verb agreement
    B. Tense agreement
    C. Ambiguous antecedent
    D. Punctuation

Questions 34-37 refer to the following passage:

Whose woods these are I think I know.
His house is in the village, though;
He will not see me stopping here
To watch his woods fill up with snow.

My little horse must think it queer
To stop without a farmhouse near
Between the woods and frozen lake
The darkest evening of the year.

He gives his harness bells a shake
To ask if there is some mistake.
The only other sound's the sweep
Of easy wind and downy flake.

The woods are lovely, dark, and deep,
But I have promises to keep,
And miles to go before I sleep,
And miles to go before I sleep.
   —Robert Frost

34. According to the narrator, why does he not stay to watch the snow longer?

 A. His horse is anxious.
 B. He is afraid the homeowner will see him.
 C. He is afraid of the dark.
 D. He has somewhere else he needs to be.

35. Which type of stanza does this poem employ?

 A. Quatrain
 B. Couplet
 C. Sestet
 D. Quintain

36. The last two lines of the poem employ which literary technique?

    A. Alliteration
    B. Repetition
    C. Free verse
    D. Personification

37. The rhyme scheme for each of the first three stanzas of this poem can be described as

    A. ABAB
    B. AABB
    C. AABA
    D. ABCA

38. Which of the following types of writing should NOT include the author's personal opinion?

    A. Journaling
    B. Expository writing
    C. Poetry
    D. Persuasive writing

39. Which of the following is NOT considered a conjunction?

    A. But
    B. For
    C. At
    D. Or

40. "Please pick up the book that's _____ the desk." What type of word would best complete this sentence?

    A. Preposition
    B. Conjunction
    C. Noun
    D. Adjective

41. "Lydia was feeling sick and dragged herself out of bed energetically." Which part of this sentence should be changed for it to make sense?

   A. Proper noun
   B. Adverb
   C. Action verb
   D. Preposition

42. "Will you come to the party this weekend?" is an example of which type of sentence?

   A. Interrogative
   B. Exclamatory
   C. Imperative
   D. Declarative

43. Which of the following is true of second-language learners developing their English literacy?

   A. They should be encouraged to use English exclusively and not their native language.

   B. Most second-language learners find comprehending English easier than producing it.

   C. Visual aids are not especially helpful to second-language vocabulary acquisition.

   D. Their literacy skills in their first language will not help them in learning English.

44. The most common organizational structure for a narrative is

   A. cause and effect
   B. sequential
   C. problem-solution
   D. persuasive

45. A child who writes "I herd the anamuls make lots of noyz" is exhibiting which stage of writing development?

   A. Conventional spelling
   B. Random letters
   C. Phonetic spelling
   D. Letter-like forms

46. "Teacher picked up book off of floor." This sentence is missing

   A. articles
   B. verbs
   C. prepositions
   D. nouns

47. In the writing process, which step follows revising?

   A. Publishing
   B. Creating a rough draft
   C. Editing
   D. Prewriting

48. Identify the error in the following sentence: "George is a real estate agent and Tony is an insurance salesman. He has been with his company for ten years."

   A. Subject-verb agreement
   B. Ambiguous antecedent
   C. Capitalization
   D. Punctuation

49. "Because the forecast called for rain later in the day, I brought an umbrella with me." What type of sentence is this?

   A. Simple
   B. Compound
   C. Complex
   D. Compound-complex

50. In order to be considered a sentence, a group of words must at least contain

A. a noun and a verb

B. a noun and a conjunction

C. a verb and a conjunction

D. a noun and an adverb

51. The understanding that words are made up of letters that have different sounds is known as

A. phonemic awareness

B. the alphabetic principle

C. the logographic foundation

D. syllabication

52. Which of the following is NOT an appropriate way to correct a run-on sentence?

A. Separate the two independent clauses with a semicolon.

B. Separate the two independent clauses into two separate sentences.

C. Join two independent clauses with a conjunction.

D. Separate the two independent clauses with a comma.

Question 51 refers to the following passage:

"Autumn"
Shades of orange and red
Leaves gently swirl to the ground
Crispness in the air

53. The poem above is an example of a(n)

A. acrostic

B. haiku

C. cinquain

D. elegy

54. Which of these is used to measure fluency?

    A. Accuracy

    B. Rate

    C. All of the above

    D. None of the above

55. "She was as tall as a giraffe" is an example of a(n)

    A. onomatopoeia

    B. simile

    C. metaphor

    D. foil

56. Protagonist and antagonist are the two main types of

    A. settings

    B. conflicts

    C. narrators

    D. characters

57. Which of these is considered an abstract noun?

    A. Donor

    B. Money

    C. Generosity

    D. Check

58. Mr. Brown assigns his class fifteen minute presentations on a research topic. Which of the following should his students do during their presentations in order to be as effective as possible?

    A. Read a prepared speech word for word

    B. Look directly at Mr. Brown throughout the presentation

    C. Make eye contact with various members of the audience

    D. Stand perfectly still

59. "Manuscript," "transcription," and "descriptive" share a common

    A. prefix

    B. suffix

    C. end rhyme

    D. root word

60. Which of these singular nouns is NOT correctly paired with its plural form?

    A. House - Houses

    B. Mouse - Mouses

    C. Box - Boxes

    D. Ox - Oxen

61. Identify the indirect object in the following sentence: "Maria loaned her book to Lauren."

    A. Maria

    B. loaned

    C. book

    D. Lauren

62. Which of these is NOT an example of a secondary source?

    A. A textbook

    B. An encyclopedia

    C. A research article

    D. An autobiography

63. Identify the helping verb in the following sentence: "Until she brings her grades up, Sydney will be grounded."

    A. brings

    B. will

    C. be

    D. grounded

64. Recognition of rhyme and print awareness are components of

    A. logographic foundation
    B. emergent literacy
    C. decoding
    D. fluency

65. The logographic foundation refers to the ability to

    A. utilize phonics to sound out words
    B. recognize sight words
    C. understand that printed letters represent sounds
    D. spell phonetically

Mathematics

66. *1, 4, 9, 16, 25...*
    What is the next number in this sequence?

    A. 29
    B. 39
    C. 36
    D. 44

67. $x^0 =$

    A. x
    B. -x
    C. 1
    D. 0

68. Using a spinner with equal segments numbered 1-6, what is the probability of a spin landing on an even number?

    A. 1/6
    B. 1/3
    C. 5/6
    D. 1/2

69. Solve for x: -4x < 16

   A. x > -4
   B. x < -4
   C. x < 4
   D. x > 4

70. The school store sells notebooks and pencils. The ratio of sales today was 2 notebooks to 3 pencils. If the store sold 6 notebooks today, how many pencils did they sell?

   A. 3
   B. 9
   C. 6
   D. 12

71. On a recent test, five friends had scores of 88, 92, 76, 94, and 80. What was the mean of their scores?

   A. 84
   B. 86
   C. 88
   D. 18

72. Which of the following would yield a result that is undefined?

   A. 12 ÷ 0
   B. 10 * 0
   C. 0 ÷ 11
   D. 5 * 0

73. If a car travels at 55 mph, how far will the car travel in 2 hours and 30 minutes?

   A. 140 miles
   B. 175 miles
   C. 12,650 miles
   D. 137.5 miles

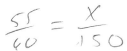

74. Which of these numbers is the smallest in value?

    A. .39

    B. .317

    C. .3564

    D. .4

Question 75 refers to the following:

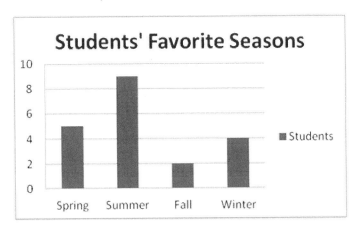

75. How many more students like summer than fall?

    A. 7.0

    B. 11.0

    C. 8.0

    D. 3.0

76. On a recent test, five friends had scores of 88, 92, 76, 94, and 80. What was their median score?

                                                     76 80 88 92 94

    A. 86

    B. 88

    C. 94

    D. 90

77. Line A contains the points (2, 4) and (4, 6). What is the slope of the line?

    A. 1
    B. 2
    C. -1
    D. 1/2

78. The set [1, 4, 16, 64...) is what type of sequence?

    A. Arithmetic
    B. Geometric
    C. Triangular
    D. Fibonacci

79. For lunch on Wednesday, students have a choice of pizza or a peanut butter and jelly sandwich. For a drink, they can choose milk, chocolate milk, orange juice, or apple juice. How many combinations of main dishes and drinks are possible?

    A. 6
    B. 4
    C. 8
    D. 12

80. The additive inverse of 4 is

    A. 1/4
    B. 1
    C. 4
    D. -4

81. An angle that measures 100° is considered

    A. acute
    B. obtuse
    C. straight
    D. right

82. **Two lines that never intersect are**

    A. perpendicular

    B. complementary

    C. parallel

    D. supplementary

83. **The product of two numbers is 12. The difference of these numbers is 4. What is the larger of the two numbers?**

    A. 4

    B. 6

    C. 12

    D. 3

84. **The Pythagorean Theorem is used to find**

    A. the slope of a line

    B. the volume of a cylinder

    C. the sides of a right triangle

    D. the midpoint of a line segment

85. **The measure of the angle that is supplementary to a 70° angle is**

    A. 110°

    B. 20°

    C. -70°

    D. 30°

86. **A quadrilateral with only one pair of parallel sides can be classified as a**

    A. trapezoid

    B. parallelogram

    C. rhombus

    D. rectangle

87. What is the absolute value of -10?

    A. 10

    B. -10

    C. 1/10

    D. 1

88. 2 is the only even number that is also

    A. rational

    B. prime

    C. natural

    D. irrational

89. Mrs. Nelson's class is 72% male. If there are 25 students in the class, how many students are females?

    A. 18

    B. 10

    C. 7

    D. 17

90. $3 + 4(1+3)^2 =$

    A. 67.0

    B. 112.0

    C. 100.0

    D. 13.0

91. To solve $2(5 + 3)^2 - 10$, the first step would be to

    A. Multiply 2 by 5

    B. Square the 3

    C. Add 5 and 3

    D. Subtract 10

92. There were 25 questions on a spelling test. If Kristen got 21 of them correct, what was her score expressed as a percentage?

    A. 21%
    B. 84%
    C. 96%
    D. 74%

93. A store buys t-shirts from the manufacturer in cases of 25 for $50. They sell the shirts for a price of $8 each. How much of a profit will the store make on the sale of 80 shirts?

    A. $480
    B. $640
    C. $590
    D. $30

94. One of the angles in an equilateral triangle has a measure of

    A. 90°
    B. 30°
    C. 60°
    D. 45°

95. Which of the following is NOT considered a prenumeration concept?

    A. Pattern recognition
    B. Informal counting
    C. Relative magnitude
    D. Arithmetic operations

96. What is the least common multiple (LCM) of 4 and 5?

    A. 20
    B. 5
    C. 1
    D. 45

97. The greatest common factor (GCF) of 15 and 18 is

    A. 3

    B. 90

    C. 5

    D. 18

98. The multiples of 6 include

    A. 1, 2, and 3

    B. 3, 6, and 9

    C. 6, 12, and 18

    D. .6, 6, and 66

99. Which of the following is NOT a factor of 16?

    A. 16

    B. 32

    C. 8

    D. 2

100. $a^2 * a^3 =$

    A. a^6

    B. a^5

    C. a^{-1}

    D. $a^{2/3}$

101. Which of these fractions is equal to 0.875?

    A. 9/10

    B. 7/8

    C. 6/7

    D. 11/12

102. Which of the following best illustrates the commutative property?

    A. 4 + 2 = 2 + 4
    B. (2 + 4) + 3 = 2 + (4 + 3)
    C. 2(4 + 3) = (2 * 4) + (2 * 3)
    D. 4 − 2 = 2 − 4

103. The area of a right triangle whose sides measure 3 cm, 5 cm, and 4 cm is

    A. 6
    B. 7.5
    C. 10
    D. 12

104. Which of these numbers is NOT equivalent to the others?

    A. 1/2
    B. 0.5
    C. 2/6
    D. 0.50

105. Which of the following is does NOT describe the number 98?

    A. Real
    B. Rational
    C. Prime
    D. Composite

Social Studies

106. Which region of the United States is marked by a hot, dry climate?

    A. New England
    B. The Southwest
    C. The Southeast
    D. The Northwest

107. Hawaii is an example of a(n)

    A. peninsula

    B. inlet

    C. archipelago

    D. country

108. Individual citizens have the least influence on government policy in a

    A. democracy

    B. republic

    C. parliamentary system

    D. autocracy

109. Which civilization was responsible for the world's first written law code?

    A. Sumer

    B. Egypt

    C. Babylon

    D. Aztec

110. Which of these is NOT considered a reserved power under the United States Constitution?

    A. Professional licensing

    B. Establishing schools

    C. Levying an income tax

    D. Marriage laws

111. Which of the following was NOT one of the primary motivations for European exploration of the Americas?

    A. A desire to convert native populations to Christianity

    B. Looking for a new source of slaves to replace the African population

    C. To find new sources of raw materials

    D. International competition for prestige

112. Which of these has the longest single term length in the U.S. government?

A. President
B. Vice-President
C. Representative
D. Senator

113. The Gadsden Purchase, the Mexican Cession, and the Louisiana Purchase were part of the United States'

A. belief in Manifest Destiny
B. New Deal programs
C. 20th century imperialism
D. Cold War era policy

114. The earliest civilization on the Indian subcontinent formed along which river?

A. Huang He
B. Tigris
C. Euphrates
D. Indus

115. Which of these climates is most likely to experience four distinct seasons throughout the year?

A. Polar
B. Tropical
C. Temperate
D. Dry

116. One advantage the American troops had over the British in the American Revolution was

A. more skilled soldiers
B. better weaponry
C. familiarity with the landscape
D. larger numbers of troops

117. Latin America is an example of a

    A. continent

    B. country

    C. biome

    D. region

118. A country that exports more than it imports is said to have

    A. a market economy

    B. inflation

    C. a favorable balance of trade

    D. a shortage of consumer goods

119. Which of these was NOT one of the primary underlying causes for World War I?

    A. Imperialism

    B. Militarism

    C. Fascism

    D. Nationalism

120. Which of these had the most significant impact on the size of the United States?

    A. Louisiana Purchase

    B. Gadsden Purchase

    C. Mexican Cession

    D. Seward's Folly

121. A student looking for the elevation of a mountain should use which type of map?

    A. Political

    B. Topographic

    C. Climate

    D. Historical

122. Which of these had the most direct influence on the adoption of the Thirteenth Amendment to the U.S. Constitution?

   A. The women's suffrage movement

   B. The end of Reconstruction

   C. Union victory in the Civil War

   D. Manifest Destiny

123. The Federalist Papers were designed to

   A. convince people to ratify the U.S. Constitution

   B. draw support for the American Revolution

   C. promote the cause of abolition

   D. specify which powers are delegated to the federal government

124. In a laissez-faire system, economics are driven by

   A. government planning

   B. collective decision-making

   C. market forces

   D. regulatory action

125. A matriarchal society is one in which

   A. men are considered superior to women

   B. the eldest female leads the family

   C. all marriages are arranged

   D. religion and government are closely tied

126. A topographic map would be most useful for

   A. calculating the population density of New York City

   B. finding the elevation of Beijing

   C. seeing how the borders of Poland have changed over time

   D. identifying the major agricultural products of France

127. Congressional approval of the President's Supreme Court nominees best illustrates the constitutional principle of

A. federalism

B. flexibility

C. checks and balances

D. personal liberty

128. The delta of the Mississippi River connects to what larger body of water?

A. Gulf of Mexico

B. Lake Michigan

C. Pacific Ocean

D. Missouri River

129. The earliest civilizations formed

A. in mountainous regions

B. democratic societies

C. extensive trade networks

D. in river valleys

130. Which of these was NOT one of the original Thirteen Colonies?

A. New York

B. New Hampshire

C. Vermont

D. Georgia

131. The United States' first attempt at a national government was

A. the Constitution

B. the Declaration of Independence

C. the Articles of Confederation

D. the Bill of Rights

132. The region of the United States best known for its grain production is the

    A. Southwest

    B. New England

    C. Mid-Atlantic

    D. Great Plains

133. A society that produces only what it needs for survival has a

    A. planned economy

    B. socialist economy

    C. subsistence economy

    D. open economy

134. Which of the following is true of ancient Greece?

    A. Most city-states had direct democracies.

    B. Most Greeks were monotheistic.

    C. Greece was a unified nation during this time period.

    D. Greece had a decentralized government.

135. The New Deal was a response to

    A. severe economic downturn in the 1930s

    B. the pursuit of equal rights for African-Americans

    C. Soviet aggression during the Cold War

    D. the bombing of Pearl Harbor

136. Hernan Cortez, Francisco Coronado, and Henry Hudson

    A. were Founding Fathers of the United States

    B. were important leaders in the American Revolution

    C. were European explorers of the Americas

    D. were military leaders in World War II

137. Plantation farming was common in which colonial region?

    A. The South

    B. New England

    C. Mid-Atlantic

    D. Midwest

138. Two of the main causes of the Civil War were

    A. slavery and states' rights

    B. boundary disputes and states' rights

    C. slavery and taxation

    D. taxation and boundary disputes

139. Humans, more than any other species,

    A. are dependent on their environment

    B. alter their environment

    C. don't use the resources from the natural environment

    D. are unaffected by environmental factors

140. Kevin is looking at a map of Pennsylvania and wants to know the distance from Philadelphia to Pittsburgh. Which of the following will he need to use?

    A. Compass rose

    B. Legend

    C. Scale

    D. Elevation

"The history of the present King of Great Britain is a history of repeated injuries and usurpations, all having in direct object the establishment of an absolute tyranny over these States…In every stage of these oppressions, we have petitioned for redress in the most humble terms: Our repeated petitions have been answered only by repeated injury. A prince whose character is thus marked by every act which may define a tyrant, is unfit to be the ruler of a free people… We, therefore, the Representatives of the united States of America, in General Congress, Assembled, appealing to the Supreme Judge of the world for the rectitude of our intentions, do, in the name, and by authority of the good people of these Colonies, solemnly publish and declare, that these United Colonies are, and of right ought to be free and independent states; that they are absolved from all allegiance to the British Crown, and that all political connection between them and the State of Great Britain, is and ought to be totally dissolved."
–Second Continental Congress, 1776

141. This document served to justify

   A. the American Revolution
   B. the Civil War
   C. World War II
   D. the Cold War

142. At the time that it was written, which of the following would have been most likely to agree with the statements in this document?

   A. A loyalist
   B. A patriot
   C. A member of Parliament
   D. A monarch

143. Tundra, alpine, and taiga are examples of

   A. biomes
   B. climates
   C. regions
   D. landforms

144. Which of the following bodies of water is man-made?

A. English Channel

B. Erie Canal

C. Hudson Bay

D. Nile River

145. Which of the following fields is the study of humans, past and present?

A. Geography

B. Anthropology

C. Archaeology

D. Psychology

146. Which of these civilizations was the first to use a civil service exam?

A. India

B. China

C. Mesopotamia

D. Egypt

147. Terrace farming is an example of

A. an important agricultural technique in used in prairies

B. a way humans have adapted to their environment

C. a characteristic of river valley civilizations

D. a practice tied to religion

148. Filial piety is best described as

A. value placed on children above all else

B. obedience and respect for elders

C. devotion to a deity

D. the careful use of natural resources

149. In his Farewell Address, President George Washington advised the United States to

A. abolish slavery immediately

B. avoid permanent alliances with foreign countries

C. create a strong two-party political system

D. ratify the Articles of Confederation

150. Manifest Destiny was used to justify the United States'

A. practice of slavery

B. Revolutionary War

C. territorial expansion

D. involvement in World War II

151. A major cause of the American Revolution was

A. conflict with Native Americans

B. Manifest Destiny

C. taxation without representation

D. division over the issue of slavery

152. The immediate cause of U.S. entry into World War II was

A. the sinking of the Lusitania

B. the Zimmerman telegram

C. the use of the atomic bomb

D. the bombing of Pearl Harbor

153. The caste system affected social relations in _____ for centuries.

A. China

B. India

C. Egypt

D. Iraq

154. The 1st Amendment includes all of the following EXCEPT

A. freedom of speech

B. the right to peacefully assemble

C. the right to petition the government

D. the right to bear arms

155. Which of these terms refers to the limited nature of resources which drives economics?

A. Surplus

B. Scarcity

C. Demand

D. Tariff

156. The last half of the twentieth century in the United States was most shaped by

A. disputes over the issue of slavery

B. competition with the Soviet Union

C. the desire for territorial expansion

D. military conflict with Germany

157. Which of these was NOT a direct result of the Industrial Revolution in the United States?

A. The population became more urbanized.

B. Manufactured goods became more widely available and less expensive.

C. Big businesses were subject to strict government regulations.

D. Factories employed many immigrants for low wages.

158. Aqueducts were an important feature in the architecture of

A. the Indus Valley Civilization

B. Egypt

C. Rome

D. Sumer

159. Confucianism was a philosophy that originated in

A. India
B. China
C. Greece
D. Rome

160. Sumerian cuneiform is most similar to which aspect of ancient Egyptian society?

A. Papyrus
B. Pyramids
C. Hieroglyphics
D. Pharaohs

Science

161. The law of superposition helps scientists to calculate

A. the velocity of objects in motion
B. the age of rock layers
C. tension force
D. the pressure of atmospheric layers

162. Which of these objects would make the best conductor?

A. A wooden rod
B. A plastic spring
C. A rubber tire
D. A wire coat hanger

163. The phases of the Moon are most directly a result of

A. the Moon's rotation on its axis
B. the Moon's revolution around the Earth
C. Earth's revolution around the sun
D. the tilt of the Earth on its axis

164. **Which simple machine would be most useful for moving an object across a long horizontal distance?**

   A. Pulley
   B. Lever
   C. Wedge
   D. Wheel and axle

165. **The most specific taxonomic classification of organisms is**

   A. genus
   B. kingdom
   C. family
   D. species

166. **Which of these types of water movement in the water cycle does NOT involve a phase change?**

   A. Melting
   B. Surface run-off
   C. Transpiration
   D. Evaporation

167. **The planet closest to the sun is**

   A. Earth
   B. Venus
   C. Mercury
   D. Neptune

168. **The force present in a wire, cable, or cord when forces pull on both ends is known as**

   A. normal force
   B. gravity
   C. tension force
   D. air resistance

169. In an ecosystems, top consumers transfer energy to

    A. primary consumers

    B. producers

    C. decomposers

    D. secondary consumers

170. The idea that an object in motion will stay in motion unless acted upon by an outside force is known as

    A. sublimation

    B. velocity

    C. inertia

    D. friction

171. Multiplying mass times acceleration will allow you to calculate

    A. velocity

    B. force

    C. weight

    D. speed

172. Which of these is ALWAYS true of an object in equilibrium?

    A. It is at rest.

    B. It is in motion.

    C. The resultant of all forces acting on the object is zero.

    D. It is subject only to normal force.

173. Weather is most directly influenced by

    A. the rock cycle

    B. the water cycle

    C. the Moon

    D. Earth's rotation on its axis

174. Which resource would be most useful in finding the atomic weight of an element?

    A. An almanac
    B. A periodic table
    C. An atlas
    D. A thesaurus

175. Which type of rock is formed by the cooling of magma?

    A. Sedimentary
    B. Igneous
    C. Metamorphic
    D. Cretaceous

176. Which of these is most directly responsible for the changing of the seasons?

    A. Earth's rotation on its axis
    B. Earth's revolution around the sun
    C. Moon's revolution around the Earth
    D. The tilt of the Earth

177. Natural selection contributes to biological evolution by

    A. ensuring that mutations favorable for survival are passed down through reproduction
    B. eliminating all mutations from the gene pool
    C. providing a means for weaker organisms to survive and reproduce
    D. ensuring that only dominant traits can be genetically inherited

178. Which of the following is NOT a characteristic of all living things?

    A. Made of cells
    B. Have definite life spans
    C. Use energy
    D. Sexual reproduction

179. The North Pole of a magnet will repel which pole of another magnet?

A. North

B. South

C. East

D. West

180. The least dense state of matter is

A. gas

B. liquid

C. solid

D. plasma

181. The speed of vibrations has the most influence on a sound's

A. pitch

B. amplitude

C. timbre

D. quality

182. Condensation involves a phase change from

A. solid to liquid

B. gas to liquid

C. liquid to gas

D. gas to solid

183. Which of these can disrupt the balance of an ecosystem?

A. Habitat destruction

B. Introduction of invasive species

C. Depletion of one species

D. All of the above

184. The common effects of stimulants include all of the following EXCEPT

  A. a high followed by a crash
  B. slowed responses
  C. irritability
  D. restlessness

185. Light is blocked from hitting the Moon during a

  A. lunar eclipse
  B. solar eclipse
  C. meteor shower
  D. Moon phase

186. Human beings belong to the taxonomic kingdom of

  A. protista
  B. animalia
  C. plantae
  D. monera

187. The food chain describes the

  A. method of energy transfer through an ecosystem
  B. ratio of producers to consumers in an ecosystem
  C. way that food moves through the digestive system
  D. nutritional value of basic food groups

188. The esophagus is part of which human body system?

  A. Respiratory system
  B. Digestive system
  C. Nervous system
  D. Reproductive system

189. **Which part of a plant is responsible for reproduction?**

   A. Stem
   B. Roots
   C. Leaves
   D. Flower

190. **The nucleus of an animal cell**

   A. produces chlorophyll
   B. is surrounded by a rigid wall
   C. contains DNA
   D. All of the above

191. **Meteorites are found**

   A. within the Earth's atmosphere
   B. in the asteroid belt
   C. near the sun
   D. nowhere in this solar system

192. **Human beings emerged during the**

   A. Paleozoic Era
   B. Precambrian Era
   C. Mesozoic Era
   D. Cenozoic Era

193. **An object's weight on Earth may be different than its weight on another planet. This is the result of**

   A. inertia
   B. friction
   C. gravity
   D. normal force

194. A paleontologist is most likely to study

    A. the skeletal remains of a dinosaur

    B. pottery left by an ancient civilization

    C. constellations

    D. weather patterns

195. The overall charge of the nucleus of an atom is

    A. negative

    B. positive

    C. neutral

    D. dependent on the element

196. Light emits

    A. radiant energy

    B. potential energy

    C. nuclear energy

    D. kinetic energy

197. Fission involves

    A. the joining of atomic nuclei

    B. the splitting of atomic nuclei

    C. the destruction of energy

    D. the creation of energy

198. Which of these is NOT a required step in the Scientific Method?

    A. Formulating a hypothesis

    B. Drawing conclusions

    C. Data collection

    D. Peer review of results

199. If two parents display the same recessive trait for eye color, the chances of the offspring also displaying the recessive trait are

    A. 0%
    B. 25%
    C. 75%
    D. 100%

200. Which of the following requires chemical bonding of its different component parts?

    A. Mixture
    B. Element
    C. Solution
    D. Compound

201. Fossils are most likely to be found in

    A. sedimentary rock
    B. igneous rock
    C. mantle
    D. the exosphere

202. The amount of solar radiation a location receives is influenced by

    A. the longitude of the location
    B. the position of the Moon
    C. the tilt of the Earth
    D. Plate tectonics

203. Animal and plant cells both contain all of the following EXCEPT

    A. mitochondria
    B. chloroplasts
    C. nucleus
    D. cytoplasm

204. Which of the following helps reduce the risk of disease?

    A. Proper nutrition

    B. Vaccination

    C. Personal hygiene

    D. All of the above

205. Which of these organizations of space is the largest?

    A. Galaxy

    B. Universe

    C. Solar system

    D. Asteroid belt

206. One result of convergent plates is

    A. the creation of new crust

    B. the creation of new bodies of water

    C. the creation of volcanoes

    D. the separation of continental and oceanic plates

207. Which of these is NOT a form of thermal energy?

    A. Conduction

    B. Convection

    C. Radiation

    D. Mechanical

208. The human body system responsible for the transport of blood is the

    A. respiratory system

    B. musculoskeletal system

    C. circulatory system

    D. nervous system

209. Which of the following has had the most long-term impact on the Earth's physical landscape?

A. Weather patterns

B. Biological evolution

C. Earth's rotation

D. Plate tectonics

210. The outermost layer of the Earth is called the

A. outer core

B. mantle

C. inner core

D. crust

Answers and Explanations

1. D

All of these are important considerations when evaluating media sources.

2. C

Identifying a topic sentence is an example of literal, not critical, comprehension.

3. C

Editorials are opinion pieces and are a form of persuasive writing.

4. D

All of these accurately describe characteristics of these lines. "Sorrow" and "morrow" demonstrate end rhyme, "Good night" is repeated, and the entire passage is written in iambic pentameter.

5. C

In this scene from a play by William Shakespeare, one character is speaking directly to another. This is called dialogue.

6. B

Puppetry is a form of drama usually intended for a children's audience. It uses dialogue to convey the story.

7. D

A diary is a type of primary source, which is a firsthand account of events from a person who witnessed them.

8. D

These are all examples of narratives, which tell a story.

9. C

Poetry is writing that is in verse, while prose is not written in verse.

10. B

An oxymoron is a phrase that combines two words with opposite meanings.

11. B

An idiom is a phrase that has come to have a different meaning through usage than the meanings of its individual words. Different languages have very different idioms and because it is difficult to ascertain the meaning of an idiom from the words it contains (without the prior cultural background knowledge), idioms can be particularly tricky for second language learners.

12. A

An antecedent is a noun for which a pronoun stands in. In this sentence, "she" is the pronoun, which refers to the antecedent "Julia."

13. B

Hyperbole is the use of exaggeration to make a point. The speaker has not literally been in line forever. The exaggeration is meant to convey that the speaker has been in the line for a very long time.

14. C

Persuasive writing expresses an opinion and makes an argument. An editorial is an opinion piece in a newspaper or magazine.

15. C

Affixes are prefixes and suffixes added to the beginning or end of base words to change their meaning.

16. A

Personification is attributing human characteristics to a non-human object, such as stars dancing, which is a human action.

17. C

Consonance is the repetition of consonant sounds anywhere within the words.

18. B

Interrogative sentences ask a question and end with a question mark.

19. A

An omniscient narrator is able to describe the thoughts of any character. First person narration is in an "I" voice, while second person uses "you." Limited omniscient is a third person narrator who can only convey the inner thoughts of one character.

20. B

Eye contact helps a speaker to know that he or she has the audience members' focus.

21. D

The climax of a story is where the conflict reaches a head and the story has its turning point.

22. C

A persuasive essay is one in which the author tries to convince the reader of a certain point of view. The only one of these sentences that expresses an opinion rather than a fact is C.

23. B

Tom is very discouraged by the prospect of painting the whole fence and is very reluctant to do so.

24. D

"Gladness left him" proceeds "melancholy" and sets gladness up as the opposite of melancholy. As the gladness left, melancholy (sadness) took its place.

25. C

The comparison of how little fence Tom has painted compared with the unpainted fence ahead helps to show how large and daunting Tom found this task to be.

26. C

Since this group of words contains no verb, it can only be classified as a phrase.

27. D

All of these actions are important components of active listening.

28. C

Free verse poetry contains neither rhyme nor meter.

29. A

Phonological awareness is the understanding that words are made up of sound units. Rhyming and segmenting are two of its associated skills.

30. C

The sentence should read "Lily and I went on vacation together."

31. D

Letter-sound correspondence is the knowledge of the sounds that are associated with each letter of the alphabet. This is essential before any of the other skills can develop.

32. B

Literal comprehension means that the student understood what happened in the story. Critical comprehension would involve analyzing the story for deeper meanings.

33. B

Tense should be consistent when talking about the same time period. "Moved," "lived," and "works" do not all maintain the same tense.

34. D

The last quatrain tells why the narrator moves on. He has made promises to someone that require him to continue to travel many more miles.

35. A

Each stanza contains four lines, which makes it a quatrain.

36. B

The last two lines are identical and make use of repetition.

37. C

This poem contains end rhyme. In these stanzas, the last words of lines 1, 2, and 4 rhyme, while line 3 contains a different ending sound.

38. B

Expository writing is meant to be informative.

39. C

"At" is a preposition.

40. A

This sentence requires a preposition such as "on" or "under."

41. B

The adverb "energetically" does not make sense with the rest of the sentence.

42. A

Interrogative sentences ask questions.

43. B

For most second-language learners, it is easier to understand written or spoken English than it is to actually speak or write the language themselves.

44. B

A sequential organization presents events in chronological order. The is the most common structure for a narrative.

45. C

These words are written out like they sound (phonetically) instead of with correct spelling.

46. A

The sentence is missing articles such as "a" or "the."

47. C

Revising is making changes to content. This step is followed by editing, which is correcting mechanical issues.

48. B

It is unclear from this sentence whether the pronoun "he" refers to George or Tony. This makes the antecedent ambiguous.

49. C

A complex sentence contains one dependent and one independent clause.

50. A

A sentence must contain a noun and a verb.

51. B

The alphabetic principle is the understanding that words are made up of letters that have different sounds.

52. D

Commas cannot be used to correct run-on sentences.

53. B

A haiku is a three-line poem whose lines measure 5, 7, and 5 syllables.

54. C

Both rate and accuracy are measures of the fluency of reading.

55. B

A simile is a comparison that uses "like" or "as."

56. D

A protagonist is the main character or hero. An antagonist works against the protagonist.

57. C

An abstract noun refers to an idea or concept rather than a concrete person, place, or object.

58. C

An important part of engaging an audience while speaking is making eye contact.

59. D

All of these share the common root "script" which means "write."

60. B

The plural of "mouse" is "mice."

61. D

The indirect object is the one that is receiving the action of the verb. In this case, the book is being loaned TO Lauren, making her the indirect object.

62. D

An autobiography is a person's account of his or her own life, making it a primary source.

63. B

Helping verbs are paired with another verb (in this case, "be") and are often used to indicate tense.

64. B

Emergent literacy refers to the language development that occurs before a child can read or write words. These skills are developed from birth and include listening, speaking, memory, recognizing pattern and rhyme, print awareness, critical thinking, and the development of the fine motor skills necessary for writing.

65. B

The logographic foundation of literacy involves the recognition of common sight words, which involves the use of visual cues.

66. C

This is a set of perfect squares.

67. C

Any number raised to the 0 power equals 1.

68. D

The even numbers in this set are 2, 4, and 6. That means that there are 3 favorable outcomes out of 6 possible outcomes. The probability of getting an even number is 3/6, which reduces to 1/2.

69. A

Remember to switch the inequality sign when dividing each side by a negative number.

70. B

Solve by setting up a proportion.

71. B

To find the mean, add up the scores and divide by the number of scores (5).

72. A

Dividing by zero always yields a result that is undefined.

73. D

Convert 2 hours and 30 minutes to 2.5 hours. 55 miles per hour multiplied by 2.5 hours equals 137.5 miles.

74. B

When comparing decimals, move from left to right. A, B, and C all have a 3 in the tenths place. In the hundredths place, choice B has a 1, which is the smallest of the given values.

75. A

9 students like summer the best and 2 students like fall the best. $9 - 2 = 7$

76. B

To find the median, put the scores in numerical order. The median is the number is the middle. In order, the numbers read: 76, 80, 88, 92, 94. The number in the middle is 88.

77. A

The slope formula is $\frac{y_2 - y_1}{x_2 - x_1}$.

Plug the points in to solve.

$m = \frac{6-4}{4-2} = \frac{2}{2} = 1$

78. B

To get from one member of the set to the next, multiply by 4. A set whose rule is solely multiplication is called a geometric set.

79. A

You can solve this problem by drawing a tree diagram of the possibilities, by listing out the possible combinations, or by using multiplication. 2 choices for sandwiches multiplied by 3 choices for drinks equals 6 possible combinations.

80. D
The additive inverse of a number is its equal opposite such that the two numbers added together would equal zero. 4 + (-4) = 0

81. B
Angles that measure between 90° and 180° are considered obtuse.

82. C
Lines that never touch are parallel. Perpendicular lines intersect at a right angle. The terms complimentary and supplementary refer to angles, not lines.

83. B
The two numbers are 6 and 2. 6 * 2 = 12 and 6 - 2 = 4.

84. C
The Pythagorean Theorem is $a^2 + b^2 = c^2$, where a and b are the lengths of the legs of a right triangle and c is the length of the hypotenuse.

85. A
Supplementary angles add up to 180°.

86. A
A trapezoid has one set of parallel sides. All of the other figures listed have two pairs of parallel sides, which classifies them as parallelograms.

87. A
Absolute value is a number's distance from zero and is always a positive number.

88. B
A prime number can only be divided evenly by itself and 1. 2 is the only even number that is prime because every other even number can be divided by 2.

89. C
72% of 25 is 18 (25 * 0.75 = 18). That means there are 18 males in the class. To find out how many females there are, subtract the number of males from the total.

90. A
It is important to follow the order of operations (PEMDAS).

91. C

The first step in the order of operations is to take care of operations within parentheses.

92. B

21/25 * 100 = 84

93. A

If 25 shirts cost $50 from the manufacturer, the cost per shirt is $2. For 80 shirts, the cost would be $160. The sale price per shirt is $8, which comes to $640 for 80 shirts. Profit = price - cost. $640 - $160 = $480

94. C

All sides and angles of a triangle are equal therefore each angle in an equilateral triangle must equal 60°.

95. D

Prenumeration concepts are elements of math-related reasoning that a child develops prior to any formal mathematical knowledge. These include all of the choices listed, except for algebraic operations, which is a true mathematical concept that must be taught.

96. A

The only one of these choices that is a multiple of 4 and 5 is 20.

97. A

The factors of 15 are 1, 3, 5, and 15. The factors of 18 are 1, 2, 3, 6, 9, and 18. The greatest common factor is 3.

98. C

Multiples are the result of multiplying a number by positive integers. 6 * 1 = 6; 6 * 2 = 12; 6 * 3 = 18; etc.

99. B

32 is a multiple of 16, not a factor.

100. B

The product rule of exponents states: $a^n * a^m = a^{n+m}$.

101. B

7/8 = 0.875

102. A

The commutative property states that in a multiplication or addition problem, the order of the numbers being added or multiplied does not affect the final result.

103. A

The formula for the area of a triangle is *A =1/2 bh*. In this case, the triangle is right so the two shorter sides will represent the base and the height. (The longest side in a right triangle is always the hypotenuse.) (1/2) * 3 * 4 = 6

104. C

2/6 is equal to 1/3. All of the other choices are equal to 1/2.

105. C

98 has factors other than itself and 1, so it is not prime.

106. C

The American Southwest is known for its hot, dry climate.

107. C

Hawaii is an archipelago—a chain of islands.

108. D

Republics and parliamentary systems provide the people with representatives and a democracy allows citizens to vote. People have very little say in an autocracy, in which the government is run by a single authoritarian ruler.

109. C

The Babylonians created the Code of Hammurabi, the first written law code.

110. C

Reserved powers are those held only by the states. Income taxes are levied by both the state and federal governments, making that a concurrent power.

111. B

European slave traders drew primarily from Africa and brought the slaves to the Americas.

112. D

Senators have the longest single term length, at six years. Presidents and vice-presidents serve four-year terms, while members of the House of Representatives serve for two year terms.

113. A

Manifest Destiny was the belief that the United States should extend from the Atlantic to the Pacific. These territorial acquisitions helped the nation to reach that goal.

114. D

The Indus Valley civilization was the first in India.

115. C

A temperate climate has warm, wet summers and cool, dry winters. Variations over the course of the year make this climate the most likely to experience four distinct seasons—spring, summer, fall, and winter.

116. C

Americans had the advantage of fighting on their own soil and the familiarity with the landscape gave them an advantage over the British.

117. D

Latin America is a region, sharing common geographic and cultural characteristics.

118. C

The balance of trade refers to the ratio of exports to imports that a country has over a period of time. A favorable balance of trade is one in which a country exports more than it imports.

119. C

Fascist regimes came to power in Europe after World War I and their rise was a cause of World War II.

120. A

The Louisiana Purchase caused the United States to roughly double in size.

121. B

Elevation (how high land is above sea level) is shown on a topographic map.

122. C

The Thirteenth Amendment abolished slavery and was adopted soon after the Civil War.

123. A

The Federalist Papers were written following the Constitutional Convention to convince people to support the ratification of the newly drafted Constitution.

124. C

In a laissez-faire system, the government is completely hands-off and market forces such as supply and demand are allowed to freely control the economy.

125. B

A matriarchy is led by the mother or eldest female.

126. B

Topographic maps are physical maps that show elevation.

127. C

To balance power among the branches, each branch of the national government has powers that are meant to limit the powers of the other branches. This is known as checks and balances. The need for congressional approval limits the president's power to appoint anyone he wants to the Supreme Court.

128. A

The Mississippi Delta is located in Louisiana and connects the river to the Gulf of Mexico.

129. D

The earliest civilizations formed along rivers due to the presence of fertile soil and water for transport.

130. C

Vermont was not one of the Thirteen Colonies.

131. C

The newly formed United States created its first government under the Articles of Confederation. It was ineffective and later replaced by the Constitution.

132. D

The Great Plains are known as the "breadbasket" of the United States due to their grain production.

133. C

A subsistence economy is one in which the people produce only what they need to survive.

134. D

In ancient times, Greece was not a single unified nation, but rather a collection of independent city-states.

135. A

The New Deal was President Franklin D. Roosevelt's domestic program designed to help the economy recover during the Great Depression of the 1930s.

136. C

All of these were explorers from Europe.

137. A

Due to the warm climate and rich soil, agriculture thrived in the Southern colonies and large-scale plantation farming became common.

138. A

Prior to the Civil War, the country became divided over the issue of slavery and the fact that the Southern states felt that the federal government was infringing on states' rights by placing limits on slavery.

139. B

While other animals adapt to their environments, humans have the ability to change their environments. Modern technology increasingly allows this.

140. C

Scale is used to show how distances on a map compare to real-life distances.

141. A

The Declaration of Independence listed the reasons for the American Revolution and declared the United States a new nation, independent from Britain.

142. B

A patriot (a supporter of the American Revolution) would have supported this document, the Declaration of Independence.

143. A

Biomes are large areas that have distinct sets of plant and animal life that are well-adapted to the environment. Biomes are classified according to geography and climate.

144. B

By definition, a canal is a man-made waterway.

145. B

Anthropology is the study of humans, past and present. Geographers study physical features, archaeologists study artifacts of past societies, and psychologists study the human mind and behavior.

146. B

The Chinese implemented a civil service exam to ensure that government employees were qualified.

147. B

Terrace farming is an adaptation that humans have made to allow them to farm on mountainsides.

148. B

Filial piety is respecting and obeying parents and other elders. Filial piety is an important aspect in many cultures around the world.

149. B

Washington thought that the best way to stay out of wars and protect the young nation's sovereignty was to avoid alliances with other nations.

150. C

Manifest Destiny was an idea that became popular in the 1800s that the United States was destined to expand its territory all the way across the continent to the Pacific coast.

151. C

One motivation for the American Revolution was that colonists were upset that the British were levying new taxes on them when they had no representatives in Parliament, who passed the tax laws.

152. D

The United States entered World War II on the side of the Allies after Japan, an Axis power, bombed the U.S. naval base at Pearl Harbor, Hawaii in 1941.

153. B

The caste system was the rigid traditional social class system in India, closely tied to Hinduism.

154. D

The right to bear arms is in the 2nd Amendment.

155. B

Scarcity of resources means that resources are limited. How limited supplies of resources are to be allocated is foundational to economics.

156. B

From the end of World War II until the dissolution of the Soviet Union in 1991, United States foreign policy was primarily driven by its Cold War competition with the Soviet Union.

157. C

Big business was fairly unregulated in the 19th century, which led to much abuse. Regulations to protect consumers were put into place in the 20th century.

158. C

Aqueducts—structures used to transport water—were an important part of ancient Roman architecture.

159. B

Confucianism was created in China by Kong Fuzi (Confucius).

160. C

Both cuneiform and hieroglyphics were early forms of writing.

161. B

The law of superposition states that the oldest rock layers are on the bottom and newer layers form on top. This helps scientists to determine geological age.

162. D

Metal is the best conductor. The other materials are considered insulators because electricity cannot easily pass through them.

163. B

The Moon takes 28 days to revolve around the Earth, during which time its position determines how it will appear from Earth and gives it distinct phases.

164. D

A wheel and axle is the most helpful simple machine for moving an object across a horizontal distance. Pulleys and levers are more useful for vertical distances, while wedges are used for cutting or splitting.

165. D

The taxonomic classifications (in order) are kingdom, phylum, class, order, family, genus, and species.

166. C

In surface run-off, water remains in liquid form. Run-off occurs when the soil becomes oversaturated with water and the excess comes to the surface and flows over land.

167. C

Mercury is the closest planet to the sun.

168. C

Tension force is the force present in a wire, cable, or cord when forces pull on both ends.

169. D

A top consumer is an animal that is at the top of the food chain, meaning it is not prey for any other animal. When the animal dies, its energy will be transferred to decomposers who process the dead tissue and return it to the Earth.

170. C

The idea that an object in motion will stay in motion and an object at rest will stay at rest unless acted upon by an outside force is known as inertia. This is part of Newton's First Law of Motion.

171. B

Force = mass * acceleration

172. C

Equilibrium is achieved when the resultant of all forces acting on an object is zero. This means that the object could either be at rest or in unaccelerated motion.

173. B

The water cycle is responsible for precipitation, which is a major component of weather.

174. B

Information about the elements can be found on the periodic table.

175. B

Igneous rock is formed when magma cools and hardens.

176. B

The Earth's annual revolution around the sun is most responsible for the seasons.

177. A

Natural selection is the process by which those traits that are beneficial to organisms are produced and passed on in the species. Natural selection is based on a premise of the "survival of the fittest," which says that those organisms best genetically equipped to survive and reproduce will and will have their traits passed on. Those organisms that are weaker will eventually die off and with them, their less favorable traits.

178. D

Some organisms use sexual reproduction, while others utilize asexual reproduction.

179. A

Magnets have two poles- North and South. Like poles repel and opposite poles attract.

180. A

Gases are the least dense. The particles move rapidly and spread to take the volume of their container.

181. A

The faster the vibrations, the higher the pitch.

182. B

Condensation occurs when a gas cools enough to change into a liquid.

183. D

Any of these factors can disrupt the delicate balance of any ecosystem.

184. B

Slowed responses are a common effect of depressants.

185. A

In a lunar eclipse, the Earth is directly between the sun and the Moon, blocking light from hitting the Moon.

186. B

Humans are classified as *animalia* (animals).

187. A

The food chain shows how energy gets from producers (plants) that make energy to consumers (animals) that get the energy through eating plants and other animals.

188. B

The esophagus transports food from the mouth to the stomach.

189. D

The flower is the site of reproduction in plants.

190. C

The nucleus of an animal (or plant) cell contains the organism's DNA.

191. A

"Meteorite" is the name given to meteoroids once they enter Earth's atmosphere.

192. D

Primates, including human beings, emerged during the Cenozoic Era of Earth's history, which is the current era.

193. C

Gravity, the force that pulls smaller objects toward a much larger one, such as a planet, is what is responsible for weight. Weight varies on different planets due to different levels of gravitational pull.

194. A

Paleontologists study fossils.

195. B

The nucleus of an atom contains protons, which have a positive charge, and neutrons, which have a neutral charge, making the overall charge of the nucleus positive.

196. A

Radiant energy is the energy of electromagnetic waves such as light.

197. A

Fission is the splitting of atoms. Fission is the type of reaction used to create atomic bombs and nuclear reactors.

198. D

While peer review can be helpful, it is not an essential step in the Scientific Method.

199. D

For a recessive trait to be displayed, the offspring must have two genes for the recessive trait. If both parents have only recessive genes, the offspring will also have the recessive genes.

200. D

A compound is the result of chemical bonding of two or more elements.

201. A

Sedimentary rock is formed from compressed sediments, including sand, other small rocks, and fossils.

202. C

The tilt of the Earth on its axis determines how direct the solar radiation a location receives will be.

203. B

Only plant cells contain chloroplasts, which are the site of photosynthesis.

204. D

All of these help to prevent the spread of disease.

205. B

The largest is the universe. The universe contains galaxies, which contain solar systems, which may contain asteroid belts.

206. C

Convergent plates are plates that collide, which can result in the creation of volcanoes.

207. D

Mechanical energy is not a form of thermal (heat) energy.

208. C

The circulatory system transports blood throughout the human body through veins and arteries.

209. D

The movements of the plates that make up the Earth's crust have shaped the Earth's landscape over time.

210. D

The crust is the surface of the Earth on which life exists.

Made in the USA
Middletown, DE
08 January 2015